EuroMarketing

EuroMarketing

*How to market products
and services in the European Union*

A practical guide for small
and medium-sized companies

Office for Official Publications
of the European Communities

Office for Official Publications of the European Communities
2 rue Mercier, L-2985 Luxembourg
and
Kogan Page Limited
120 Pentonville Road
London N1 9JN

© European Communities, 1997

First published in 1997

This publication may only be reproduced, stored or transmitted, in any form or by any means, with the prior permission in writing of the copyright-holder. Within the UK, exceptions are allowed in respect of any fair dealing for the purposes of research or private study, or criticism or review, as permitted under the Copyright, Designs and Patents Act, 1988.

British Library Cataloguing in Publication Data
A CIP record for this book is available from the British Library.

ISBN 0 7494 2042 1 (Kogan Page Limited)

ISBN 92 827 6504 0 (Office for Official Publications of the
 European Communities)

Typeset by Northern Phototypesetting Co. Ltd., Bolton
Printed and bound in Great Britain by Biddles Ltd, Guildford and King's Lynn

CONTENTS

		Page
Foreword		*9*
Introduction		*11*

Chapter 1 **The Single Market, Does It Affect My Company?**   **15**
    The million dollar question   15
    Ask yourself   18
    Disappearing barriers to trade   19
    The new European home market   19

Chapter 2 **Becoming Informed**   **25**
    Starting your research   25
    Product strategy   26
    Pricing strategy   26
    Distribution strategy   27
    Promotion strategy   28
    Do-it-yourself research – a checklist   29

Chapter 3 **Towards EuroMarketing**   **31**
    The EuroMarketing concept   31
    Now ask yourself   35

Chapter 4 **One Marketing Strategy for the European Home Market**   **36**
    Targeting European consumers   36
    One marketing policy   37
    What your competitors are doing   37
    Why standardise EuroMarketing policies?   38
    An integrated approach   38

Chapter 5 Knowing Your Customers and Competitors   **42**
      Ciberveu: taking the temperature of its
         customers 42
      Ask yourself 46
      Finding out about your market and
         competitors 47
      Target your customers 49
      The US experience 51
      Using an integrated approach 53
      Actions to take 54

Chapter 6 Positioning   **59**
      Getting a piece of the cake 59
      Ask yourself 63
      Developing a positioning statement 64
      To do 68
      Your positioning statement for Europe 70

Chapter 7 Product Policy   **71**
      Diekirch: the quality taste for Europe 71
      Case study – Mobalpa 74
      Remaining barriers to product
         standardisation 77
      Ask yourself – product development 79
      Developing your EuroProduct 80

Chapter 8 Pricing Policy   **87**
      Pricing 87
      Things to do 91

Chapter 9 Sales and Distribution Policy   **94**
      Sales and distribution 94
      SMEs in the US 96
      Ask yourself – in the light of the information
         given 101
      Your distribution document 102

Chapter 10	**Promotional Policy**	**104**
	Brand building and advertising 104	
	What you should ask yourself – and do 106	
	Choosing agencies 108	
	Checklist for choosing a consultancy 108	
	A consistent message throughout Europe 109	
	To do 117	
	Ask yourself 117	
	Your branding strategy for Europe 118	
	The timetable for completing your branding strategy 119	
Chapter 11	**Developing, Implementing and Evaluating Your EuroMarketing Strategy**	**120**
	Rolling out 120	
	Organising for Europe 124	
Chapter 12	**In Conclusion**	**126**
	EuroMarketing 126	
Appendix A	**The Single Market: An Update by Sector**	**128**
Appendix B	**Euro Info Centres: A Contact List**	**135**
Index		*193*

FOREWORD

by

Michel Vanden Abeele

Director-General, Directorate-General for Enterprise Policy, Distributive Trades, Tourism and Cooperatives (DG XXIII), European Commission

Among the most important challenges facing DG XXIII, which is responsible for enterprise policy within the European Commission, is to help small and medium-sized enterprises (SMEs) to take full advantage of the opportunities arising from the creation of a Single Market within the European Union. This is not through the provision of subsidies, or other actions which might distort competition, but by assisting them to overcome those difficulties arising mainly because of their size and relative lack of resources.

We are conscious of the heavy burdens imposed on the management of smaller enterprises and the resultant shortage of time in which to learn about, and take advantage of, management techniques in common use in the larger business. It is our understanding that marketing falls firmly within this category.

To take full advantage of the Single Market, firms with suitable products or services and the capacity to do so need to be able to enter new geographical markets. This is recognised to be an expensive exercise and can result in failure, or perhaps very limited success, unless a systematic approach is taken.

In order to try to assist this process, a decision was taken to carry out research into current best practice in this field and to use the findings as the basis of a step-by-step guide to what has been conveniently termed 'EuroMarketing'. As with all general guides it needs to be used with common sense, always bearing the specificities of your company in mind. It is hoped that the guide, which is based on case studies of successful marketing exercises by SMEs, and is written in a form which should allow you to reach your own conclusions, will stimulate ideas and help you to adopt a unified and effective approach to conquering new markets.

Michel Vanden Abeele

INTRODUCTION

The European Single Market is now virtually complete. There is a need for all businesses, down to the very smallest, to examine the implications this has for them, not least in terms of marketing their products and services.

This introductory guide endeavours to set out a structured approach to what is conveniently called 'EuroMarketing', a process designed to assist businesses to progressively expand into new markets in other countries within the European Union in a consistent and cost effective manner. It has been written on the basis of evidence gathered from managers of small and medium-sized enterprises (SMEs) from across the European Community and in the USA. Why so many examples from the USA appear is because SMEs in that country have had a long experience of expanding from their own marketing region into others within a single market. The lessons to be learned appear to be of direct relevance to European managers who are trying to come to grips with the changing business environment in which they operate. This research has revealed some companies which are already reaping the benefits of the Single Market and others still struggling with its implications. The objective has been to turn what has been learned into a practical tool for use by SME proprietors and managers.

The EuroMarketing guide

The intention is to help you devise your own EuroMarketing strategy to the extent this makes economic sense. Therefore, the guide basically consists of:

- examples of relevant marketing strategies, with lessons to be learned;

- guidance on the use of the marketing techniques referred to in the text;
- questions designed to help you assess your company's marketing opportunities;
- pointers as to how to take full advantage of a market of 370 million people.

What this guide will not do for you

The guide will not remove the need to consider the financial implications of the decisions you make as a result of using it, nor to ask for professional advice on a series of issues that will arise. Not being based on a rigid methodology it cannot provide answers to your questions, only guidance. Only you have sufficient knowledge of your company to provide them.

So, the intention is to help you to ask the right questions about your company, about the products or services you offer, about the competition, about customers and about the way you should market your products or services. Do remember, however, that marketing is not an exact science but an important modern business tool. Its use should help you better develop your business, but the final assessments and decisions will still have to be yours, and must not be taken in isolation from other factors, such as availability of finance, production capacity etc. In addition, it will be necessary, given the rapidity with which the overall business scene continues to change, to consider other issues not directly connected to the Single Market. For example: developments in the field of informatics; the increased pace at which products become obsolescent; and the increased globalisation of business with the market changes this brings about.

Is EuroMarketing for you?

Your company may well have prospered by selling only to your local, regional or national market. The closeness to your customers – often one of the main strengths of SMEs – should help you to fight off competition, but you need to be aware of potential threats to your position. It is likely that some competitors, new or existing, will start to employ EuroMarketing techniques, trying to serve an ever larger market, reaping the benefits

Introduction

of their increased scale and rationalising the sales process. They will become fierce competitors as a result and you should be prepared to meet the challenge.

Also, should your company become really successful, you may become tempted to expand into neighbouring territory. In this case you had better weigh up the consequences. The survey of European businesses did not reveal any areas of activity which have not already, or will soon, become open to the use of EuroMarketing. Collective buying and promotion, network marketing and franchising even affect the local butcher, to name just one example.

Despite this, you may eventually decide that the EuroMarketing approach is not feasible for your products and services. Even so, it is hoped that using this guide will still give you some pointers into ways in which you can improve your current marketing methods.

How to make the most of this guide

In each section we will be asking you to respond to questions and collect information about:

- your own company;
- your competitors;
- your customers.

We suggest answering these questions in writing, very briefly and within the given space. Your own answers will lead you to a better understanding of the opportunities and threats that exist and actions you might take.

Never forget the need to 'benchmark' the performance of your company as well as your marketing strategy against those of your competitors, both actual and potential. This is vital if you are to develop a realistic company strategy.

CHAPTER 1

THE SINGLE MARKET, DOES IT AFFECT MY COMPANY?

The million dollar question

As stated earlier the legislative framework underpinning the Single Market is now virtually complete. In assessing its impact on your company it is important not to take too narrow a view. In an era of increasingly rapid technological change there would still be major challenges to face even if it did not exist. Considering this factor, together with increasing public concern with respect to environmental pollution and the quality of life, not to mention the search for individuality and the protection of the European heritage in an increasingly impersonal world, no one involved in business management can safely ignore the need continually to restructure and adapt. Add to this the opportunities and threats posed by the Single Market and the imperative becomes an urgent necessity.

While it is difficult to obtain comparable statistical data, the researches conducted by the European Observatory for SMEs already indicate the progressive development of a 'Single Market' effect. This is most clearly manifesting itself in an increase in the value of trade between member countries of the European Union. Not only this, the number of smaller enterprises which are exporting is increasing steadily. In addition, the progressive internationalisation of markets is forcing a growing number of SMEs, particularly those in sectors involving technological innovation, to launch products at home and on export markets simultaneously.

These developments could have a profound impact on your business

EuroMarketing

and you need to know what these are likely to be and how you should react to them. In order to do so, and before becoming deeply immersed in this book, you are advised to start by assessing where your company stands in the market compared with, say, five years ago. Is its position improving, static or declining? How are your principal competitors of five years ago progressing *vis-à-vis* your own company? Have any new competitors entered the market in that period? If so, do they present a material threat to your position? Answering these questions can help you to identify any direct 'Single Market effect' on your business but remember, even if none can be detected today, this may not be valid for the future and it would be unwise to leave matters there. There may also be other European level legislation, particularly in the field of the environment, which could have a direct effect.

Even so, this is not as easy an exercise as it may at first appear. For many small companies it is virtually impossible to determine their position in the market precisely, their percentage share being too small to calculate, even though they may be exploiting a valuable and profitable niche. In fact, for many SMEs, market size is probably not significant of itself. What is more important is the view taken by customers and suppliers of your standing and prospects. It is essential to go and ask them, even if on occasion the replies are unpalatable.

The answers should also be measured against your future aspirations for the business, providing indications as to whether or not these are achievable without changes being made to its operations. This should be accompanied by a standard SWOTS (strengths, weaknesses, opportunities, threats) analysis, leaving you with a clear idea as to what operational areas require attention. Before undertaking any reorganisation it is essential that you consider the effects of the Single Market and the actions you should take in response. The use of this guide should help you to take a structured approach when considering the marketing aspects.

A warning

Many owners of small businesses are totally unclear as to where they would like it to be in five years' time. Neither do they have a credible and up-to-date business plan. Nor do they even know what business they are actually in, concentrating on the product they are supplying (whether goods or a service) rather than on the need they are satisfying. This is a recipe for living from day to day, spending the majority of one's time dealing with emergencies. You really should be able to give positive answers

The Single Market

to the three questions asked below before going further with this exercise.

1. What business am I in?
2. Where do I want to be in five years' time?
3. Does all this accord with my business plan?

If you have never drawn up a business plan, use this exercise as your incentive to create one. You do need it, just as much as you need proper budgets and cash-flow forecasts, together with accurate management accounts that enable you to compare actual outturns against predictions. To operate a business without these essential tools is like going on a motoring holiday without a road map. Existing business plans will almost certainly need to be revised in the light of the decisions taken during the present exercise but this should follow on logically.

If you are now in a position to proceed please turn to the next page and ask yourself...

EuroMarketing

Ask yourself

How do you define your home market?

- Has competition for your product/service increased over the last two years?
- How many companies were you competing with five years ago in your home market?
- How many companies are you now competing with?
- Of these, how many are located in other European Community countries?
- What was your market share nationally, or your position in the market five years ago?
- How large is your market share now nationally?
- What are the reasons for the change (if significant)?
- What percentage of your turnover went to EC countries at that time?
- What percentage goes there today?
- What are the reasons for the change?
- How important a factor has European market integration been to your company?
- How does the reduction of physical and technical barriers to trade affect your business?
- Do European competitors pose a direct threat for you at the moment, if so how?

If you do not know the answers to any of the above, the information given in the following pages may help.

Disappearing barriers to trade

The objective of the Single Market programme, as far as business was concerned, was to allow the free movement of goods, services, people and capital by doing away with existing barriers to trade between the Member States. This policy was intended to be at the heart of efforts to safeguard the competitiveness of European industry, to create jobs and to stimulate economic growth.

Some 280 different pieces of legislation were involved. To describe them all, together with their potential impact, would require a separate book, but the principal ones, together with the progress made, are described briefly in Appendix A. The intention is to enable you to decide on those which are of greatest relevance to your operations because of the actual or potential opportunities or threats they pose. Only sufficient information is given to help you to do this. To provide more than broad indications would present the danger of the information becoming rapidly outdated and, therefore, misleading. In order to evaluate the impact fully, direct and indirect, it will obviously be necessary to obtain further and more detailed information on what you determine are the most critical sectors as far as you are concerned.

The key message is that, taken as a whole, the Single Market is working, even if there are problems in specific areas. The removal of border controls is being reflected in greater efficiency and lower costs for European business, capital is moving freely between Member States and more firms, although not yet enough, are competing in public procurement markets. Nevertheless, you do need to know where potential difficulties could arise as a result of the process being incomplete in order to be able to see how others have overcome them.

Finally a word of warning. Do not become so immersed in an examination of the legislative structure applying to the market that you forget one basic truth. In the end, and unless it turns out there are insuperable technical barriers to surmount, which is unlikely, it will be the merits and demerits of your product, and the way in which you market it, which will determine the degree of success achieved.

The new European home market

The creation of the European Single Market, coupled with the more gradual, but still significant effects of greater European integration, are

EuroMarketing

already having a profound influence on marketing concepts in a number of sectors. Some European companies, anticipating change, have already changed their trading outlook in so far as the European Union (EU) is concerned. To them there are no longer any 'foreign' markets in Europe, simply a European market which they supply.

Developing marketing plans which take into account this larger market is sensible, even for smaller firms. Only companies doing this will be fully able to enjoy the Single Market's benefits, to the extent their individual circumstances allow. In undertaking this exercise it is important to understand the underlying objectives of the Single Market programme. The aim was not to create a homogeneous market but one which was more integrated.

This is likely to result in the emergence of further regional markets on the pattern of those already existing in the Benelux and the British Isles. Possible examples are ones encompassing Portugal and Spain, and South Sweden, Denmark and Northern Germany. This will still leave clear differences in patterns of consumption between Northern and Southern Europe, not to mention between the more and the less economically developed regions.

Single Market benefits include:

- easier physical access to markets in other countries;
- lower costs due to the elimination of frontier controls and the simplification of administrative procedures;
- lower costs due to improved economies of scale;
- a greater opportunity to exploit comparative advantages;
- increased innovation and dynamism as a result of liberalisation, freer competition and increased cross-border business.

These benefits should make it easier for you to penetrate new markets, but for smaller companies it is important not to attempt to do too much. Rationalisation by larger organisations should create new openings, but these are likely to be in niche markets. It is these which need to be identified.

Marketing trends in Europe

Among the first companies to change their marketing strategies for the integrating Europe were the foreign multinationals, partly because of misplaced fears about the creation of a 'fortress' Europe. Most large companies had already revised their marketing strategies well before the actual coming into being of the Single Market. Even smaller firms can learn from an examination of what has been done by such companies in terms of product, pricing, distribution and promotional policies.

It should also be remembered that larger firms are concentrating production of a product group within one European plant. At the same time they are diversifying their purchasing, searching for the best suppliers of components across Europe. This is leading to a higher proportion being sourced across borders. This can create major new opportunities for those firms equipped and prepared to seize them.

Products

The progressive removal of technical and other barriers, either through mutual recognition of products or through harmonisation of different standards, opens the door to the launch of more standardised 'Euro-products'. That is, brands sold in more than one country but employing a common marketing position, strategy and package design, but with differences in labelling for legal reasons and recipe, or other, variations. They will certainly become more common, but products which are marketed across Europe with totally harmonised specifications will still remain in the minority. What will be more significant will be the appearance of a greater number of partially standardised products, each seeking to exploit a series of niche markets on the basis of a common positioning strategy.

This will be bound to increase competitive pressures on existing products in the same field, leading producers, as a result, to allocate proportionately more marketing effort to their primary products at the expense of marginal items in their range. Manufacturers of mainstream brands that are only distributed in one single market, which are not focused in their positioning and do not therefore enjoy a loyal customer base, will be especially vulnerable as trade barriers come down. This movement towards greater concentration on a core range of products can provide the opportunity for smaller firms to exploit the niche markets that are created as a direct result.

Pricing

Currently prices for the same product can still differ widely from one EC country to the next. Cross-border variations in price are often due to different product positioning and distribution strategies on the part of the producers and to differences in consumer awareness, coupled with varying degrees of competition. The practice of using different strategies for different countries is expected to decrease progressively.

This is because parallel imports, cross-border procurement alliances and mergers among distributors will reduce manufacturers' ability to charge different prices for the same product between EU countries. Excepting indirect tax effects, the internal market reforms should also help to reduce cross-border price spreads on the same item.

Distribution

Speciality retailers will continue to meet the needs of similar consumer segments throughout Europe with a common brand name and marketing formula. At the same time, retailers, distributors and brokers, currently operating in only one market, are forming cross-border alliances to consolidate their buying power. This could necessitate major changes in current distribution methods by suppliers seeking to meet their requirements.

With mutual recognition, even with all its current imperfections, many smaller manufacturers will be looking to sell standard products outside their home markets to supplement domestic sales of their branded products. As a result, the availability, quality and price competitiveness of private label goods is likely to grow. Pan-European franchising is also likely to increase following the removal of trade barriers.

In addition, the end of restrictions, for example those which previously required financial services firms to have individual national regulatory approval and a registered office in each EC country in order to market their products, is likely to fuel the growth of direct mail, telephone marketing and other non-traditional distribution channels. Nevertheless, the current legal restrictions imposed on these activities in some countries have to be taken into account.

Finally, the absence of border formalities will increase the scope for rationalising physical distribution channels.

Promotion

It is predicted that an increasing proportion of advertising expenditure will be placed in pan-European media. Media buyers estimate that firms marketing their products and services across Europe will eventually spend

25–50 per cent of their media budgets in pan-European media. There are important savings to be made if identical, or similar, advertising materials can be used in a series of markets. Furthermore, directives have been proposed to unify broadcasting codes throughout the EC. This may facilitate the development of pan-European advertising plans.

Sales promotion, on the other hand, is a promotional tool still suffering from large differences in legislation between the EC member states regulating how enterprises can and cannot promote their products. As an example, games of chance, where winning a prize is completely random, are forbidden in Denmark and France, but permitted in Ireland and the UK. Games of skill on the other hand, i.e. where winning a prize takes skill and/or judgement, are permitted in France and permitted under certain conditions in Denmark. In that such rules are always subject to change it will be up to you to make yourself aware of the different restrictions currently applying in any market where you have a potential interest in selling, using such sales promotion techniques.

Henley faces the challenge

During the 1980s the Henley Centre for Forecasting was developing and enhancing its reputation as the UK's principal socio-economic forecasting agency. By applying a range of techniques – in such fields as econometric measurement, market research, time use analysis and income forecasting, the Henley Centre equipped itself to provide strategic guidance to client companies in consumer markets faced with issues of brand positioning, pricing, corporate identity and new product development. With the revitalisation of the commitment to a Single Market that occurred in the mid-1980s, it became clear to the Henley Centre that a Europeanisation of its ideas, structures and ambitions was essential to its intellectual wellbeing and long-term prosperity. The reasons for this were primarily :

- in a politically and economically integrating Europe, it was inconceivable that any one society, such as the UK, could be analysed and understood in isolation from crucial 'external' influences;

- client companies (frequently multinational corporations), themselves excited by the prospects of '1992', required services which responded to their need to perceive and understand the kind of consumer society the component nation states of Europe were becoming;

- progressive market integration justified the belief that new, non-UK customers could be found for the Henley Centre.

In short, the Henley Centre wanted to be a European company servicing European suppliers of consumer products. As a company with less than 100 employees, and based principally in London, the Centre faced a number of imperatives and options by which to pursue this objective. In essence, these were:

1. To achieve success on a European scale at minimum cost. An inexhaustible supply of long-term investment funds was not available.

2. To achieve some measure of success as quickly as possible. It was important to set reasonable short-term objectives and to maintain morale and enthusiasm by achieving prompt, even if modest, results.

3. To avoid unnecessary risks. When the Centre (in concert with Research International) launched its flagship service 'Frontiers: Planning for Consumer Change in Europe' it was not possible to carry out a costly market test, but it proved very valuable at the blueprint stage to seek the advice and reaction of existing clients in order to ascertain the market sensitivity.

4. To 'Europeanise' staffing policy. The centre's language skills were already very good, they now had to become first-rate; a decision was taken to recruit non-UK nationals whose experience both contributed to the company's current operations (and whose presence was therefore in no sense a cost) and underpinned the future attack on non-UK markets.

Once these principles had been established it became possible to address the different strategic choices facing what was and remains a small company keen to sell marketing/planning support services across languages and across business sectors and into new/different parts of Europe, but with only limited resources.

You can now begin to consider how to do the same.

CHAPTER 2

BECOMING INFORMED

Starting Your Research

More will be said on the subject of pure market research later in this book. In starting to develop a EuroMarketing strategy, however, it is important to appreciate from the outset that even when fundamental research indicates market conditions are apparently favourable, applying the same marketing strategy across the EU is only feasible if and when national legislation and administrative procedures do not create insuperable obstacles. As we have seen their removal is one of the explicit objectives of the Single Market programme, but that this process is not finished. The objective of this chapter, therefore, is to help you evaluate the number and relative severity of the non-commercial obstacles you face. In addition some hints on other aspects of research will be given.

In order to become fully informed, and remain so, you need to keep abreast of changes at national and European levels which affect the possibility of your selling in other countries the same product/service you developed for your local market, to apply the same pricing strategy, to use similar distribution channels and to support sales by similar promotional tools.

Your trade association and/or chamber of commerce should be able to provide much of this information, but do not forget the widespread range of information and assistance available from European Information Centres. In particular, try to obtain answers to the following questions regarding your product, pricing, distribution and promotion strategies.

Product strategy

While the changes wrought by the Single Market receive most attention in this book, others must be taken into account when formulating a product strategy. One example is the greater attention being focused by governments, business and consumers in environmental issues, leading to legislation on the disposal of packaging waste and the control of harmful emissions. If you are to develop an effective product policy it is important that all these issues be taken into account when deciding:

- Can your current product/service with its present specifications be legally sold in other EC countries without any changes?
- If not, what changes would be required at present?
- From what date, if relevant, will such adaptations no longer be required?

May we suggest that you tabulate the information for each category of product you offer so that you are able to refer easily to the situation applying in each Member State in which you are interested.

Please pay special attention to issues such as European standards, packaging, labelling, product liability, etc. In doing so remember that most Single Market legislation took the form of directives. The result is that, when transposing them into their own legislation, Member States were only under an obligation to meet the objectives set out. This gave scope for the interpretation of these objectives in slightly different ways. There could, therefore, be differences between legislation in one Member State and another. On occasion these could be significant.

Eventually you should end up with a list of legal and administrative obstacles standing in the way of your implementing a similar marketing approach across the European Union. In some cases this will not be important, as you may decide for good commercial reasons not to tackle the markets presenting the most significant administrative and legal difficulties for the foreseeable future. If not, it would be helpful to try to find out how your competitors have coped with these problems.

Pricing strategy

Establishing a pricing policy is one of the most vital decisions to be made. Charge too little and you will have neither sufficient profit margin nor proper scope for undertaking promotional activities. Charge too much and you are likely to limit the size of your target market and may leave yourself vulnerable to competition. Once it is established it may be difficult to change your pricing policy. This means there is a need for you to look at the current pricing levels of similar products or services in the other Member States. Nevertheless, there is no need to follow existing practice slavishly, always providing you can find justifiable reasons for taking a different approach.

In making comparisons between your existing and target markets it is important to evaluate the relative impact of factors such as taxation, value added tax (VAT), retail or customer price levels, dealer or distributor price or discount structures, the usual size of representatives commission or salesforce cost, direct sales costs (such as co-operative advertising and allowances or training) and total distribution costs on the normal pricing structures operative in a particular market. Note that in some Member States you will find that legal controls exist on the scale of discounts and other allowances granted and the ability to make special promotional offers.

Distribution strategy

- Can your current product/service be distributed in other EC countries through similar distribution channels?
- If not, what changes would be required at this moment?
- Is there any likelihood of this situation changing in the immediate future?
- If not, and significant problems have been identified, will the different methods which need to be employed invalidate a EuroMarketing approach?

In answering the above questions it is always necessary to distinguish between distribution and physical delivery of goods. In the latter instance different methods may well have to be used in different markets, but this will not undermine the validity of using a unified approach for the rest of the marketing operation. Do remember the costs of physical distribution are significant, and are too often given insufficient consideration. It is worth spending time conducting research into what appears to be the most cost-effective methods of physical distribution currently being used in a given market.

EuroMarketing

Of course, the approach finally taken will also be dependent on the actual selling method used, and here it will be particularly important to look at that used by firms of a similar size in your sector of activity. If sales are only to be made to a limited number of outlets it may be possible for these to be effected by one of your existing sales executives, but then the question of language will be important, not only for the person undertaking the actual selling, but for those other members of staff who are likely to be contacted by your customers over the telephone.

If direct selling is not possible, then a choice has to be made between a number of alternatives: establishing a sales office; appointing a sole distributor (always remembering that some markets such as Germany are divided into several distinct regions, with few distributors covering them all adequately); or, using a sales agent. Again, you should see what similar firms to your own are already doing and determine whether this is proving effective.

Please pay special attention to issues such as EC competition rules, contract law in respect of commercial agents, consumer protection, distance selling, general product safety, unfair contract terms, industrial and property rights, trade marks, copyright, etc. Also any potential taxation and social security obligations that might arise, and the legal responsibilities to be met, in respect of any branches and subsidiaries you might contemplate establishing in order to compete effectively.

Promotion strategy

- Can your current product/service be promoted in other EC countries without any changes to the promotional strategy?
- If not, what changes would be required at this very moment?

Generally speaking, questions of promotional strategies will concern market practicalities rather than legalities, although most countries have some restrictions on how certain products may be advertised and any claims that can be made, and it is important to discover the details.

Otherwise, the basic question to be asked is whether the culture and traditions in the various Member States create barriers to the implementation of a unified marketing strategy. Only you can weigh the evidence, which must be derived from thorough research, and decide this.

A checklist to assist you with your overall researches follows ...

Do-it-yourself research – a checklist

This research checklist includes the most important questions to be answered. When researching the markets get as much 'fresh' research information as possible by interviewing buyers, end-users or consumers, and obtaining as much data as you can using legitimate means concerning competitors.

The manager responsible should arrange for the collection of information on all your major markets, current or target, using this checklist. He or she should bring together all the material that you have, and in the light of the knowledge gained, answer the questions below. This is an essential stage in creating the foundations of your EuroMarketing strategy. Where no clear answer is forthcoming it will indicate the necessity of conducting additional research.

Product/service characteristics

- What are the key customer benefits?
- What is the customers' definition of value?
- What are the customer information requirements?
- What are the difficulties involved in making sales?
- What are the customer service requirements?

Channel of distribution characteristics

- What is the pricing structure and required discounts?
- What is the service and support required?
- What type of service is there to the end-customer?

Promotional requirements

- What are the major trade shows?
- What are the promotion activities required of the channel (push activities)?

- What direct-to-customer promotion activities are required (pull activities)?

Pricing

- Build a price chart of all direct competitors and substitutes. For each competitive product and direct substitute fill in the following:
  - retail or customer price;
  - dealer or distributor price or discount (if applicable);
  - representative commission (if applicable);
  - sales force cost (if applicable)
  - direct channel costs, such as co-operative advertising and allowances for training, etc;
  - total channel costs;
  - achieved margin (sales price less channel costs);
  - contribution to central overhead costs.

Customers

- How do they currently buy?
- How would they prefer to buy?

The competition

- How do they market?
- What differences are there compared with your own tactics?
- Significant product price points?
- What are their key product benefits?
- What are your products distinctive advantages?
- Disadvantages?
- What form of promotion do they use?

CHAPTER 3

TOWARDS EUROMARKETING

The EuroMarketing concept

The last chapter was concerned with the conducting of research designed to identify barriers to adopting a EuroMarketing strategy. It is now time to introduce you to the actual concept. The most helpful way to do so is to provide an example of the successful approach taken by one company and to see what lessons capable of virtually universal application can be learned.

Illycaffe: Espresso for Europe

Illycaffe, located in Trieste, a city in the Northeast corner of Italy, is a family run company that produces high quality Espresso coffee. Unlike many of its Italian competitors who have added Espresso to the other types of coffee they offer, Illy focuses solely on producing Espresso coffee and invests considerable energy into spreading a dedication to quality throughout its work force of 220. This policy has made it one of the most successful Espresso companies in Europe.

A new European vision

In 1990 Riccardo, the founder's grandson, became head of Illy's international activities as marketing director. He had a very clear idea of where the company should be heading: a more unified European market provided an excellent opportunity to launch a brand with a strong and standardised image and of a quality that would appeal to consumers across

EuroMarketing

Europe. With this goal in mind, he went to work implementing Illy's European strategy.

Steps towards EuroMarketing

Riccardo Illy decided that his first task in trying to implement a pan-European marketing programme was to create a unified team and to bring the whole structure under his direct control. He felt that the most effective way to begin this process was to buy out his distributors in each major market. This was a courageous act requiring considerable capital investment, but the company was willing to take this step in order to become fully in command of selling operations, thus facilitating the implementation of the same marketing programme throughout Europe.

Illy then concentrated on its product in an attempt to find a standardised version that could be sold across Europe. This would reduce production costs, simplify logistics, and help to create a unified image. Standardisation meant the number of different roasts had to be reduced. Illy reduced the range of roasts produced from seven to four by eliminating the darkest and the two lightest blends.

Creating a pan-European image

The success of Illy's new approach soon became obvious as sales in Europe began to take off. At the beginning of 1992, the company was ready to use advertising to promote its image as the producer of the best Italian Espresso coffee in Europe.

Illy had done very little advertising in its European markets in the past. Advertising decisions traditionally had been left to distributors and were made on a country-by-country basis, but Illycaffe now decided to cut costs as much as possible by working with a single agency and a common theme. They selected an advertising agency with experience in pan-European advertising and gave them a difficult brief: to design an advertising theme that would work in all countries, for all customer segments, and for all of the company's products. The agency came up with a successful concept that was easily adaptable to different languages, different media, and even different national symbols and tastes.

As Riccardo Illy explains:

> This would never have been possible before. We did not have the control over our distributors that would have been necessary. We did not have a European identity with the same sort of positioning in each

country that would have made the investment effective and efficient. Now we do. And the fact that we are involved with only one agency, that can hand over a standard package to its local offices for any adaptations necessary, is a tremendous saving for us both in terms of money and time. We don't have to go shopping for agencies in each country and run around trying to get them to focus on some similar idea. And we don't have to increase our staff in order to give the marketing managers time to do this job.

The time was also ripe for co-ordinating the company's public relations activities across Europe. Once again Illy looked for and found a PR agency that could handle a pan-European programme. Such a plan was made easier by the now standardised image of quality Italian Espresso and the company was again able to save co-ordination costs and time by working with a single agency on a unified image. This included the use of a common logo, and the production of cups, umbrellas and other promotional material, all bearing the same image.

The future

What is in store for the future? As barriers become further reduced Illy will most likely eliminate its warehouses throughout Europe and replace its current national distribution centres with smaller organisations dedicated only to sales. Invoicing and despatch will then be handled directly from the headquarters in Trieste. The saving that may be gained from such a change will then be reinvested to continue the process of capturing an ever larger share of the European market.

Conclusions

The Illy experience shows the importance of: maintaining control of the whole marketing operation, difficult though this may be on occasion; developing a unified image; rationalising the product range offered in other markets; and providing effective advertising and other promotional support. This lesson is applicable whatever the product or service you are marketing.

Nevertheless, theirs is a high risk strategy, depending on the continued success of what is basically one product. It may be applicable in the case of coffee, but could present dangers where either tastes change, or the structure of final distribution channels to the consumer alter or are rationalised through company amalgamations or regroupings. There is also an

EuroMarketing

even greater need to be in the forefront of technological progress if dependent on such a compact range. Finally, the proposed concentration of all European distribution and invoicing at one point could create practical problems. Factors such as these need bearing in mind when developing your strategy. Nevertheless, the overall concept, as set out in the previous paragraph, should now be clearer and possible to apply to your own operations.

Questions designed to assist follow ...

Towards EuroMarketing

Now ask yourself

On the basis of the lessons learned from the Illy experience, briefly answer the following questions. They will all be assessed more in detail in the following chapters, so it is only necessary to set down your broad tentative conclusions at this stage.

- Are you currently taking into account the realities of the Single Market?
- Do you currently sell the same product/service throughout the EU?
- Why/why not?
- Do you sell your product/service at the same price throughout the EU?
- Why/why not?
- Do you use the same brand name throughout the EU?
- Why/why not?
- Do you use the same design for packaging throughout the EU?
- Why/why not?
- Do you use the same promotional message throughout the EU?
- Why/why not?
- What are for you the benefits of selling the same product throughout the EU or, if you currently do not do this, what is the added cost of manufacturing, distributing and promoting different products?

   – benefits:
   – added costs of manufacturing:
   – added cost of distributing:
   – added cost of promotion:
   – other added costs:

CHAPTER 4

ONE MARKETING STRATEGY FOR THE EUROPEAN HOME MARKET

Targeting European consumers

Any organisation developing a European marketing strategy would be ill-advised to ignore the fact that European nations, and even regions, can still be very different from one to another. Our histories and cultural traditions have shaped habits and attitudes with their own distinct features. While we have been trading with each other as nations for hundreds of years our business cultures are still sometimes very different.

Nevertheless, these differences are not hindering companies like Illy from developing marketing strategies that tap into our similarities as consumers. Now, changes in Europe, brought about by tourism and the impact of the media as well as legislation, are making it possible for more companies to sell on the basis of a single policy throughout the EC. This can apply to both final and intermediate products and to services.

You should know your current customers well, and even the characteristics of your end-consumer where this is applicable. Knowing consumers and potential consumers of your product or service is an important place to start when thinking about how to expand your sales. The advice is to target consumers with similar characteristics, giving priority to those markets where they are most numerous, with the objective of capturing their attention and eventual loyalty through meeting the needs they have in common.

One Marketing Strategy

Current trends in consumer behaviour, when coupled with the greater availability of social research, are making it possible to distinguish certain similar attitudes, ideas and tastes across Europe. Not all consumers can be put into neat categories, but there is a strong commonality of outlook and behaviour within some groups. Companies can, and are, selling products to them specifically designed to match these characteristics.

One marketing policy

Small, and even medium-sized, companies can rarely afford the costs, let alone the administrative stress, of selling into a number of new markets at one and the same time. From hard experience you may already know all too well the initial cost of doing business in another market. Some of this expense is due to having to do things differently from at home. Even if you have not exported before you should theoretically be aware of the potential problems created by different cultures and languages; that product, packaging and labelling requirements can differ; and of the pricing complications brought about by possible fluctuations in currency values. These factors in combination normally make it too complicated and expensive for most firms to launch a marketing programme in more than one market at a time, and may have put you off from selling outside your home market altogether.

As we have already seen the situation is changing for the better, with the Single Market being designed to do away with the majority of the legislative barriers, and proposals for the establishment of a single European currency by 1999 at the latest. Dynamic companies are already preparing to take advantage of the growing opportunity these changes offer by developing one marketing policy for Europe. More and more companies are trying to make products which will satisfy customer requirements in different markets simultaneously, using the same brand name, selling them at the same price and using the same promotional message. Variations tailored to the requirements of regional or even local markets are provided only if and when no other solution can be devised.

What your competitors are doing

If you answered 'yes' to some of the questions posed at the end of the previous chapter, you are also probably already thinking about rationalising

EuroMarketing

your marketing policies to the greatest possible extent. You are not alone, many other managers are too. Their number may surprise you.

In preparing this book 754 managers of exporting businesses across the EU with less than 500 employees (small and medium-sized enterprises) were asked the same questions in a quantitative survey. Nearly all of them (98 per cent) had already adopted a standardised marketing policy in at least one of the following areas: product development, pricing, promotion, brand name and packaging.

Over one-third of the SMEs surveyed intend to increase the number of standardised marketing policies. Currently, nearly 70 per cent of the surveyed SMEs do this in three areas or more. This will increase to 80 per cent in the next two to three years. What is more, the numbers intending to do so are the same for SMEs marketing to consumers as for those marketing to other businesses.

Why standardise EuroMarketing policies?

Large and small companies are standardising because:

- it is the most effective way to address European consumers or buyers with similar tastes or requirements; discrepancies in pricing and promotion can also create long-term problems;
- it rationalises the marketing process and allows economies of scale in production, and possibly in Research and Development. Savings may also be made in the cost of producing advertising material, sales training and servicing costs;
- it creates a framework for building on accumulated experience;
- it maximises the potential of a home market of 370 million relatively wealthy consumers, an unrivalled home base from which eventually to contemplate selling worldwide.

An integrated approach

The sections of this book which follow will be devoted to helping you devise an integrated EuroMarketing plan. It will look at the different phases of conceiving a EuroMarketing strategy, with hints being given as to how you may develop each of them. The remainder of this chapter briefly introduces you to each of the concepts involved. In considering each of them do remember that your company is an SME not a multinational, with a whole range of specialised departments. Do keep it simple!

Research

Look at each market in order to determine whether a sufficient body of users exist with similar characteristics to those you already serve. Define both the similarities and the differences that exist. This is not a simple process for a smaller company, but may be made easier by studying the activities of your competitors, together with the results of social surveys that have been conducted. Nowadays the latter are incorporated into an official publication, which is updated annually, in most European countries.

Positioning

It is always important to ask the question 'What market am I in?' That is, what needs of your customers, real or perceived, are being satisfied? Unless you are clear about this it is impossible to have a well-devised marketing strategy. When you have decided this, look again at those markets where you have determined potential exists and examine whether the unique selling propositions you make use of at home are equally applicable, or whether the approach has to be modified and to what extent. Also, whether the positioning will be the same. At home you may be targeting the middle segment of the market. In less economically advanced countries you may need to aim at a more selective target.

Composing your marketing mix

With the information you now have at your disposal you should be able to determine the main thrust of your marketing effort, and the relative weight to be accorded to sales support, advertising and public relations, to mention just some of the factors to be considered. Although you will be only tackling one market at a time you still need to be certain that the marketing mix will be equally applicable when launching in subsequent markets. This may involve compromises, but these should be kept to the minimum. Otherwise you may end up with a coherent approach but one largely lacking in impact.

Product

If you have a range of products it will be vital to determine which of them will be marketable throughout the EU using basically the same product and pricing policies. It is on these that efforts should be concentrated. Should you decide to adopt new product strategies, always bear in mind that this will have an impact on existing customers in your home market. Do discuss these changes with the most significant among them, making sure that they are in agreement. Otherwise, losses of traditional business could outweigh the benefits of new business gained.

Pricing

Linking price to positioning is one of the keys to success for EuroMarketers. As has been pointed out in the section on Product Positioning, the situation could well arise where a product is fairly everyday in its home market, but treated as a speciality in others. This will mean that sales volumes will be smaller for some time to come, with selling and distribution costs proportionately higher. The eventual aim must be to see the product positioned similarly in all markets, but this will require time and considerable promotional effort. Pricing may well have to reflect this, being higher in markets other than the home market. In instances such as this it is preferable to develop a strong niche market, applying some of the extra margin to promotional activity. Prices can always be dropped later when the market begins to enlarge and competitors appear, as they eventually will. This is much easier to do than having to raise prices later because it is found that an insufficient portion of the promotional expenses are being recovered. This question will be looked at in more detail in the chapter devoted to pricing.

Distribution

It is vitally important to understand thoroughly the distribution system in the markets being targeted. The objective must be to undertake physical distribution as quickly as by domestic suppliers of products in the same category, with as low, or lower, error rate. Otherwise, all the benefits of an integrated selling and promotional programme will be dissipated. This may well be an area in which it is impossible to adopt an identical strategy for all markets, but this is of less importance than achieving effective results at an acceptable cost. Problems only really arise where there is a requirement for different forms of packaging, for example ten sales units to a display carton instead of 12. Even then it should be possible to cope with two variants without incurring major additional costs.

More important is being able to control how the product is presented to the purchaser and/or end-user. This must not be done in such a way that the central selling strategy and message is undermined. For example by attempting to sell large initial quantities of a product aimed at a select niche market. If a third party selling and distribution organisation is to be used, contractual agreements should be drawn up in a way that enables you to ensure this.

Promotion

It is important to use the same core communications concept, with the minimum of variations to suit individual market conditions. Where consumer products are involved it may well be that variations may well have to be built in to the promotional policy in order to allow for the differing requirements of retailers. Taking supermarkets as an example, some may allow you to place your point of sale promotional material in their stores, and may well require a high level of merchandising support in return. Others will only allow the use of their own promotional material, will specify the shelf space to be allocated, and may not even allow your personnel into individual stores. When researching a market it is essential to find out if such differences in merchandising policy exist and how to cope with them. Otherwise, you will be unable to apply an integrated promotional policy and may produce unsuitable material.

As you are no doubt beginning to see, your customers as well as final consumers are likely to fall into distinct groups. What is important is to adopt a trans-border approach which will satisfy the needs of each type across the EU. This is possible because the number of basic policy variations open to retailers are fairly limited. In essence they can be: top-of-the-market specialists; offer a broad product range at an apparently competitive price to the mass market (the 'one-stop-shopping' concept); or, be limited range low-cost discounters. What is important from your point of view is to have a promotional package which, while standardised, is sufficiently flexible to cope with the different ways in which retailers have developed their own market positioning and related promotional strategy.

CHAPTER 5

KNOWING YOUR CUSTOMERS AND COMPETITORS

Earlier in this book considerable emphasis was placed on the importance of obtaining market information from your existing customers and finding out all you could about the activities of your competitors. The self-same procedure needs to be adopted for each market which, following what has probably been desk research, appears to be of sufficient interest to warrant detailed investigation. While it is important to maintain a degree of secrecy about one's intentions, customer contact is also important when developing new products. One of the 754 companies surveyed provides some interesting pointers as to how this whole operation should be carried out.

Ciberveu: taking the temperature of its customers

Joseph Viladomat reveals a small white apparatus in the form of a flattened pear tucked under his shirt that repeatedly says,

Your temperature is 36.5... Your temperature is 36.5...

He smiles proudly while listening, not so much because his body temperature is correct but because the 'Voiced Thermometer' reflects the success of Ciberveu's first standard product for both the blind and the general public.

Since we began in 1989 almost all our products have been specially developed for the Spanish National Organisation for the Blind (ONCE) which is a shareholder in the company. The thermometer is the definitive leap towards economic independence.

The company and the project

Joseph Viladomat described how the company got the idea to develop the thermometer:

> In the beginning we conducted interviews with handicapped individuals to help identify new areas of development. There were many good ideas but they were always very specialised and it was difficult to judge their viability. After 1991 we concentrated our efforts more towards consumer products that might attract a broad range of consumers as well as the disabled. We changed our methods of research. The development team met periodically to brainstorm and generate ideas. The thermometer came up in one of these meetings. It was just what we were looking for.
>
> Twenty months and 535,000 ECU later, we had the prototype. We managed to develop a thermometer of an appropriate size and design that, after taking the temperature of the body over a period of two minutes, could repeat the temperature four times in whatever language was appropriate, and could be sold to the consumer for only twice the price of a simple digital thermometer.

EuroMarketing strategy

The primary marketing objective of Ciberveu was to launch the thermometer for the blind market in Benelux, Germany, Italy, Portugal, Spain and the US using a standardised approach with the same product, brand name, price and communication strategy. As Ciberveu had no experience of running a marketing campaign throughout Europe, the blind market was seen as a learning experience for duplicating a similar campaign for the general consumer market.

The process started with a market analysis to gauge the general market environment for thermometers. The research gave them crucial information required about the blind and commercial markets which they would need to develop their European and international entry strategies.

EuroMarketing

The market

Their initial research showed positive signs: no similar product existed and the market for thermometers was large. Some voice thermometers already existed on the international market, although they could not be described as personal. As an example, the one promoted by the American Association of the Blind was a device of considerable size and was sold for nearly four times their target price.

A large number of personal thermometers are sold in Europe each year. The 38 million inhabitants of Spain buy some six million thermometers per annum and the figure is similar in other countries. The biggest buyers, around two-thirds of the total, are health-care institutions that prefer the classic mercury thermometer, basically because of its low price. Concerning individual buyers, each year one personal thermometer is sold for every 20 Spanish citizens and this part of the market prefers the more expensive but easier to read digital thermometer.

Large manufacturers of personal thermometers do not exist in Europe. The majority of pharmaceutical manufacturers distribute thermometers of non-European origin, including them as complementary articles in their product range. Manufacturers' interest in thermometers as such is low and no one company wants to set off a price war without being able to guarantee its cost leadership.

Important factors

Ciberveu became aware of certain market factors which would dictate the way in which the thermometer would be launched:

1. Rival manufacturers were capable of developing similar products in the space of a year or two. Therefore, the time span for achieving sufficient market penetration and economies of scale would have to be very short.

2. While Ciberveu had sufficient capacity for research and development, it did not have the personnel, the experience or the financial resources necessary to develop a commercial and distribution network on either a European or international level. Thus the product had to be marketed via collaboration agreements with distributors in each region.

3. The Spanish National organisation of the Blind, which had supported the development of the thermometer, presided over the World Organ-

isation of the Blind. It exercised an important and influential role in decision making for member organisations and this link gave Ciberveu an advantage in the market aimed at handicapped consumers.

4. Although the thermometer was equally attractive to handicapped and ordinary customers, the intended market orientation of Ciberveu in the medium term meant that it was more likely to succeed if it targeted the handicapped market.

Faced with these market conditions Joseph Viladomat felt the conclusions were clear:

> The thermometer had to help us capture a position as suppliers of products and services for the handicapped consumer on the international market and thus make possible the general development of the business. We decided to approach the consumer market, not so much from the perspective of consolidating a position and developing it, but as a profitable operation in itself in which the domination of the process of commercialisation was of secondary importance.

Conclusions

A point should be made about the research method used for the development of the product concept. As so often happens, real consumers (blind people in this case) cannot by themselves identify better solutions for what already exists and have a hard time identifying really 'new' product concepts. By contrast, and in this particular situation, 'in-company' brainstorming is usually more useful in developing innovative products than relying on consumer research alone. Businesses developing innovative products for new markets in Europe and abroad will have to do consumer research and be creative and innovative at the same time. Never forgetting that their customers still have to be convinced.

Now, we suggest you assess the adequacy of your present levels of research into customer needs and competitor activities by answering the questions on the following pages.

Ask yourself

- **How well do you know your customers?**
- Who are your customers?
- How do you obtain information about your customers?
- Do you talk with your customers?
- At what occasion?
- Are these talks properly prepared and structured in order to maximise the usefulness of the information gained?
- **How well do you know your competition?**
- Who are your competitors?
- Who are your future competitors?
- How does your product/service distinguish itself from those of your competitors?
- How do you obtain information about your competitors?
- **What research have you been doing up until now?**
  - trade fair visits
    which?
  - visiting competitors
    which?
  - collecting information from companies
    how and which?
  - reading trade magazines
    which?
  - using trade statistics
    from which sources?
  - collecting market data
    from which sources?
  - studying market research reports
    from which sources?

Knowing Your Customers and Competitors

> - consulting trade directories
>   which?
> - hiring a market research agency
>   for what purpose?
>
> - What were the results?
>
> - What changes have you made based on the research findings?
>
> - Which research method proved most useful to you and why?
>
> - In the end, did this research help you to improve the way you sell?
>
> - *Finally:* summarise the strengths and weaknesses of your existing strategy to know your customers better and to find out about the activities of your competitors.
>
> **Now: please consider the points raised in the next section and see how these might help you to strengthen your activities in this area.**

Finding out about your market and competitors

In the old days, marketing was seen as an 'extra'. It was enough to make a good product at a cheap price and go out and sell it. Now, competition is much more fierce and customers have become more demanding. Technological expertise is not enough any more; effective marketing has become one of the keys to business success and any good marketing strategy is based on market research. Research will help you to know your market, market trends and what the competition is doing.

Gone are the days when local and regional economies could be partially immune from external influences and market trends. Progressively managed companies are making it their business to collect information on:

- the size of the market;

- how it is divided up and structured;

- significant competitors;

- market trends;
- developments in distribution channels and key buyers;
- price and discount levels;
- marketing strategies used by competitors.

Now let us see the approach to this problem of what, in international terms was a small producer of alcoholic drinks.

'The cream is real, the whiskey is real, only the taste is magic'

Baileys only launched their new alcoholic drink after three years of intensive research and development. The objective was to produce an instantly palatable liqueur that encouraged rapid consumption. The possibility of creating a market for a pleasant-tasting light liqueur was attractive for three reasons:

- first, in the liqueur market, alcohol content was discovered to be a less significant factor than taste in determining preference;
- second, a liqueur promised to be the easiest and least expensive kind of product to introduce. Market research could be carried out with little difficulty and at low cost, consumer reaction to new varieties of drink would be relatively quick to determine, and the maintenance of heavy expenditure on media advertising would not always be necessary providing the product was sufficiently unique;
- third, most established liqueurs had a low rate of consumption; they were high proof, drunk occasionally and in small quantities. Therefore the frequency of repeat sales was low – a clear disadvantage for stockists.

'Baileys Original Irish Cream Liqueur' was developed as a high priced, high quality, low alcohol, 'Irish' product of a unique character, and incorporating a new technological breakthrough – the successful blending of fresh cream and alcohol in a stable mixture. It was primarily aimed at international markets.

It was positioned as an original high quality liqueur type drink with a solid Irish heritage and a much wider consumer franchise than any other liqueur. This would establish an entirely new drink sector synonymous, and epitomised by, the brand 'Baileys'. The name was easy to say in almost any language, and was strongly differentiated from the products offered by any competitor.

An example of Baileys' advertising themes in various international markets illustrate the point: 'The cream is real, the whiskey is real, only the taste is magic'. Tasting, followed by heavy advertising, were to remain the cornerstone of the Baileys international market entry strategy throughout the world. By early 1981, Baileys was selling to more than 30 countries and territories worldwide.

Conclusions

It will be observed that Baileys could not expand market by market. This is because, as their research had shown, to produce a new variety of liqueur was relatively easy and not particularly expensive. From this they could be sure that other similar competing products would appear on the market relatively soon. If they were to capitalise on their innovative product it was essential to attack all major potential markets virtually simultaneously.

While the advice offered throughout this book is that only one new market should be tackled at a time, there are exceptions to every rule. It could be that your research will lead to the conclusion that if you expand into new markets your competitors will react quickly by offering products with similar features, even identical ones if it is impossible to obtain legal protection of your intellectual rights. They could even seek to curb your expansion by entering certain markets ahead of you.

Faced with this situation it is still probably necessary, if only for logistical reasons, to tackle one market at a time. What may have to change is your timetable for launches in further markets, with this having to be shortened considerably. If this is the situation you face, never forget the strain that rapid expansion will place on your organisation, and on its financial resources. It is better to exploit available opportunities partially but profitably than to risk the future of the organisation through reckless overambition.

Target your customers

Your European market consists of all the possible customers for your product or service throughout the EC. It is most unlikely that you can reach all of them at the same time, so you will have to decide which group

EuroMarketing

you will target. Your research should tell you the most attractive niche, ie groups of customers to target.

Successful EuroMarketers:

- identify the target customer;
- identify the consumer group, if applicable, in other regional/national markets;
- identify what customers want from their product or service in terms of need (actual or perceived: concrete or emotional).

Talk with customers

When you are selling in your own country you know your customers and your competitors quite well. They speak the same language as you do, they have the same habits. From experience you should know what customers in various categories like to buy, and how best to sell it to them. If you are now considering moving into other markets, you will probably have done a good job of selling at home.

What is automatically acceptable in your country could be totally unacceptable in another market. As mentioned previously, other countries have different habits and business cultures. This means that buying preferences will most likely be different, except perhaps in certain niche sectors. Knowing what customers want will be the key to your success. So will knowledge of your competitors, how they sell their products and promote them. One does not have to agree with their strategies, but understand them and learn from them in order to be able to sell your products and services in an effective way in their markets. You need to know your market very well, finding out what your customers want and keeping abreast of market trends. Personal visits to existing and potential customers will get you far down the road towards developing a mix which is right for your product, service, and company.

Successfully exporting companies claim that there is no substitute for making flesh and blood contact. Well targeted questions to the right people can give you much of the information you need to improve your existing operations and start exploring new markets. First, of course, you have to identify with some care who the right people are. This may require the assistance of a native of the country concerned who is experienced in the appropriate market sector.

One of the most important goals of the research is to find out whether

Knowing Your Customers and Competitors

your product needs improvement before it is ready for new markets. What do buyers and customers expect from it? Does it have a unique feature or aspect? What sort of welcome can your product hope to receive in a new territory where it has been hitherto unknown? Are there any special conditions to be observed? Will a substantial advertising budget be required before the product will be accepted? Is above or below the line advertising (media versus point of sale and public relations activity) considered more important by buyers? Even if they are not prepared to accept your brand do opportunities exist for marketing under the buyer's label? These sorts of questions, and they obviously need amending in line with the sector of activity involved, can only be clarified through carefully prepared personal visits.

These visits are too important to be left to a technician. You will have to know what your product/service will need in order to open up new markets successfully, and how to remedy any deficiencies. Managerial visits are not only a good learning tool but also good public relations. Experience shows that existing and potential buyers and end-users like to know that they are being listened to! They also wish to hold a conversation with someone they believe to be empowered to take decisions.

In order to carry out this research language skills may have to be developed, or brought in from outside. If language and culture is a problem, why not have a marketing student from a country you are interested in do a traineeship within your business? He or she can be valuable at the research and implementation phase. Another advantage is that their advice, unlike that of a distributor already engaged in the market, will not be coloured by their specific commercial interests.

The US experience

Although the US offers marketing advantages that Europe cannot – particularly one language (generally speaking) and one currency – it can provide lessons concerning marketing, and particularly the importance of personal contact when seeking to extend the area in which a product is sold. A study of the US market showed that this was a key success factor for SMEs going nationwide.

Successful small companies in the US were analysed in order to learn about how they operate in a fully integrated market. In doing this the focus was on SMEs which started selling in their local market and successfully expanded their selling nationwide. What is often referred to as

EuroMarketing

coast-to-coast marketing. Over 19 cases were analysed covering SMEs marketing consumer and industrial products.

Doing the field research personally

The one thing found common to all the successful national roll-outs (see the appropriate chapter for an explanation of this technique) was that top management, or the owners themselves, made the visits required to learn what was required. They talked to industrial buyers in their offices and met them at seminars and trade shows. They met the retail buyers if the product was to be sold through retail stores. In service businesses, they visited the competition across the country (something that is frequently less acceptable in Europe) to see how they operated and also talked to their customers.

Talk to other businesses

One example of this policy was the founder of a quick printing shop who travelled around the country talking to the owners of independent quick printing shops. The knowledge he gained was so critical to his success that he still spends several months a year visiting competitors and he has established a national trade association of quick printers.

Another concerned the owner of Oil Changers, Inc., who was trying to expand his business. He spent a year travelling around the country talking to other owners of operations supplying quick lubrication services. He learned about the latest technology, pricing, margins and growth strategies. As he continued to grow, he continued to travel, planning six trips a year. These trips were so valuable that he formed the National Association of Independent Lubricators as a national trade association providing a forum for the exchange of experience.

... and to customers

Customers collectively will give you the information on the best way to market the product. This includes what they need, what will work, whom to use as representatives and distributors where this is required. In every one of these successful cases top management did the interviewing themselves.

By the end of these visits the manager knew:

- how customers bought;
- how the participants in the appropriate distribution channels did business ;
- what the competition was doing.

Using an integrated approach

The example of Day Runner: know what the competition is doing

Day Runner, Inc. started by selling a line of time planners as executive novelties through gift shops around their base in California. In studying the competition they learned that the market was divided between two companies. One sold through its own direct catalogue mailed to most executives. The other company sold primarily through the catalogues of others; it provided a limited distribution of a limited range to office supply dealers.

The industry had grown up selling only through direct catalogues to executives who do not normally go to office supply dealers. As a result no company provided a full retail range.

Day Runner decided to fill the gap and create a full range, priced from US$25 to US$225, which was sold only to office supply dealers. This happened at a time when small companies were growing and office supply superstores expanding. This meant that company managements tended to begin making more physical purchases rather than through catalogues. As a direct result of identifying and exploiting a market trend Day Runner's policy was a success and it is now the sales leader in the market.

DTL: know how the customer buys

Another example is DTL, a manufacturer of a new energy-efficient street lighting. This company built a force of 18 independent manufacturers' sales agents with a total of 60 sales people calling on the public utilities which purchased street lights. This force was built after contact with utility buyers at direct meetings or during industry seminars. They were asked which representatives they respected, and made recommendations accordingly.

One of the first sales agents, whom the company contacted provided details of an association of manufacturers' sales agents. A list of members was acquired and half the company's selling force came from that list.

Each sales agent was interviewed personally by the company manager to learn about their strategy and to ensure that he or she knew enough to understand how difficult this new product would be to sell. A pricing policy was designed which allowed enough margin to pay above the standard rate of commission. There was also money set aside from receipts to train the representative salesforce. Without the preliminary conducting of in-depth discussions with potential customers it would have been difficult to devise a selling and pricing strategy that so exactly met market requirements.

Vornado Fans: know the distribution chain

Vornado Fans invented a high priced circulating fan. Its first sales were to a specialist catalogue, but company management knew that to achieve wide distribution for a relatively expensive product, it must sell through high class department stores. The owner visited department store buyers to determine what would make them take on the product.

It emerged that they wanted assistance in the form of co-operative advertising and a product that would sell itself rather than sales assistants having to acquire specialised product knowledge. So a programme was devised that included a 10 per cent advertising allowance, which was high by industry standards; product displays that described the advantages of the Vornado design; and, brochures attached to each fan which customers could read. A stand was also taken at the National Hardware Show in order to introduce and sell the product to visiting buyers. Although few sales were actually made at the show (which is quite normal), dozens of enquiries were received from manufacturers' representatives (agents) who wanted to market the line to department stores. From this list of enquiries a team of agents was selected. National distribution in department stores was achieved within one year without having to add any new wholly employed sales staff.

Actions to take

Establish a list of research sources for collecting the required information on competitors and potential customers in those markets from which you

Knowing Your Customers and Competitors

will select the one to be tackled initially. Again, ask help from your European Information Centre, Chamber of Commerce, government export assistance organisation and trade association to complete your list, as well as any contacts you may have in the markets concerned. Try to make a ranking of the information sources that are most important for your company on the basis of which organisations are likely to be most helpful and useful.

Organisations

European Information Centre:

_____
_____
_____
_____

Chamber of Commerce:

_____
_____
_____
_____

National Export Assistance Organisation:

_____
_____
_____
_____

EuroMarketing

Regional Export Board:

_____
_____
_____
_____
_____

Trade association (1)

_____
_____
_____
_____
_____

Trade association (2)

_____
_____
_____
_____
_____

Personal contacts

_____
_____
_____
_____
_____

Knowing Your Customers and Competitors

Trade fairs (where/when/what type):

_____
_____
_____
_____

Trade magazines:

_____
_____
_____
_____

European research sources

Also you may have to look up information in some other written sources. The following are some suggested published sources (Source: Research International).

Marketing data

- *Euromonitor – Market Reports, European Marketing Data and Statistics.*
- *European Commission – Panorama of European Industry* (provides a detailed market analysis by sector of activity)
- *Economist Intelligence Unit – Marketing in Europe.*
- Worldcasts/Predicasts, Frost & Sullivan, Canadean.
- Trade associations, trade journals and newspapers.

Market research reports

- *Directory of Market Research Reports, Studies & Surveys* (Findex).
- *Euromonitor's European Directory of Marketing Information Sources.*

EuroMarketing

- *International Directory of Published Market Research* (BOTB/Arlington).

Trade directories

- *Kompass, Dun & Bradstreet* (main ones).
- Also: *Moody's, Jane's, Kelly's*.
- *Europe's 15,000 Largest Companies*.
- Company lists produced by Fortune, Forbes, The Times.
- *Kompass Contact Europe*.
- *International Directory of Importers – Europe*.
- *Pan-European Associations*.

CHAPTER 6

POSITIONING

Definition of positioning: To juxtapose and distinguish your product in the prospective buyer's mind from your competitors.

Getting a piece of the cake

In the very south of The Netherlands lies the town of Maastricht, famous for its history, the Treaty which bears its name, and its multicultural integration. Nearly two-thirds of the EU's population lies within its 500km radius giving companies located there a major incentive to expand outside their home market, particularly as Maastricht lies virtually on the borders of Belgium and Germany. One such company is Pie Medical which manufactures medical diagnostic equipment and has 167 employees.

Pie is extremely successful with over 70 per cent of its revenue coming from sales to other European countries (Benelux, Germany, Spain, France and Italy), but like many companies it has felt the impact of foreign competition. Management eventually realised that relying on technical expertise was not enough. They had to develop a marketing policy based on solid research and concentrate on developing their European market.

Technical expertise

In 1980, Pie Medical introduced the first ultrasound scanner under its own name. Its initial success helped to establish Pie Medical's reputation as a manufacturer of diagnostic ultrasound equipment. The position of the company was further strengthened two years later by its introducing a portable ultrasound scanner, the first of its kind to appear on the market. It had the same capabilities and technical specifications as the larger, much more expensive machines.

Yearly investment in research and development amounted to almost 10 per cent of turnover, and the range of products increased. As a result Pie soon achieved an international reputation. In 1986 revenues were roughly derived in equal portions from Europe, the United States and the rest of the world.

But there were problems

Until the 1980s Pie Medical used a broad strategy, attempting to cover a considerable number of markets with a wide range of products. However, this lack of focus gradually led to an end to growth. To add to the difficulties the number of employees gradually rose. Worse yet, exports to the US also levelled off due to a decline in the company's investment in that market. Pie Medical began to lose its way: it had stagnating revenues, a set of non-strategic business units and an extensive product range.

Strategic survival

The solution decided on was a quick change in strategy – to focus only on specific, attractive segments within its target markets. The company decided to:

- focus on a familiar and relatively local market, Europe;
- choose those segments of its target market with the greatest potential;
- develop a limited set of standardised products with as few local adaptations as possible, as well as a standardised pricing and promotion policy.

Pie Medical management used a three step approach in order to focus its marketing plan:

- first, they segmented their market, dividing the market into distinctive groups of buyers who required specific products or marketing approaches;
- second, they evaluated the attractiveness of each segment in order to select one or more market segments with the best potential;

- the third step included formulating a competitive positioning for the product and a detailed marketing strategy in order to exploit properly the segments chosen.

Divide and conquer

Pie Medical's aim was to achieve a strong position in a few chosen areas of the large and somewhat fragmented ultrasound market. The typical target groups were private medical practitioners, specialists, private clinics and hospitals. However, focusing on one group meant there was a risk of a particular market segment turning sour. A wrong move could mean financial disaster, so they had to choose carefully. They started by using market research to look for an attractive market segment. This meant it should have sizeable sales potential, a high growth rate, a high profit margin, weak competition and simple distribution channel requirements.

Research sources

International exhibitions, like the MEDICA fair in Düsseldorf, were very important for making contacts and keeping up to date with developments within the industry. Market forecasts and customer surveys were used to confirm trends of which the company was already aware. Pie also maintained, and maintains, close links with hospitals and medical specialists all over the world. This enables the company to identify new opportunities in its markets and to respond quickly and effectively to developments both inside and outside its specific areas of business.

Market positioning

In addition to their own research an outside consultant was engaged, who undertook an analysis to identify where the company stood in relation to competitors in the chosen market. They found out there were about 10 major market players in Europe with Japanese and American companies posing the greatest external threat.

Following this market study Pie Medical decided to adopt a niche marketing approach, focusing on the high performance ultrasound market. The company had been a pioneer in this field and research showed that this market segment was expected to grow by 50 per cent between 1991 and 1995.

Conclusions

The example of Pie Medical was chosen to show how one company took action to focus its operations and to position its products correctly in the market. This is vitally important. If the range is too large and/or incorrectly positioned it will be difficult to convey a sufficiently powerful marketing message to key buyers. This will militate against achieving more than a marginal impact in any new market entered, unless the product or service possesses outstanding qualities or an enormous promotional expenditure. Even then, failing to secure a clear position within the market will render your operations vulnerable to competition.

While it has been impossible to give more than an outline of how Pie Medical approached this task, the questions on the next page are designed to enable you to begin to develop your own distinctive strategy, bearing in mind their experience.

Ask yourself

You should know how your goods or services stand in relation to your competitors in your national or regional market. If not, now is the time to remedy this serious defect in your operations. Even when you do, you are less likely to know how they measure up in relation to other potential European competition. More importantly, do your customers know?

At the risk of repeating what by now should be self-evident, it is suggested you answer the following questions in respect of your home market:

- Who are your customers?
- Why do they buy your product/service?
- What do they use it for?
- What is the difference between your product/service and that of your competitors?
  - (competitor 1)

  - (competitor 2)

  - (competitor 3)

Then, having decided what your existing home market positioning actually is, and once you have identified certain potential markets in other countries, ask yourself the following questions:

- Who are your potential customers?
- Why should they buy your product/service?

EuroMarketing

- How would they use it?
- Are there any differences in usage compared with your existing markets:
- What is the difference between your product/service and that of your potential competitors?
  - (competitor 1)

  - (competitor 2)

  - (competitor 3)

- What advantages/disadvantages do you possess?
  - *Advantages:* How may these be exploited?
  - *Disadvantages:* In what ways can these be overcome?

Always bearing this market information in mind, please see below for advice as to how to develop your positioning statement ...

Developing a positioning statement

You already probably know from bitter experience that having a high quality product at a reasonable price is often insufficient reason for potential customers to buy it. They need to be convinced of its merits and the added value it will bring to their business. Taking consumer products as an example, there are always far more on the market than there is shelf space to accommodate them. Buyers have to be shown the clear benefits arising from providing your product with an allocation of this scarce and valuable commodity.

Successful EuroMarketers, like those referred to earlier, have spent time and effort in defining the identity of their products and how to distinguish them from others. It is an essential part of developing an integrated approach.

Positioning

If it sounds easy, it is not. The more common the product, the more difficult it is to develop a strategy which clearly defines it from its competitors. Many companies use outside consultants to help them develop a number of positioning strategies and then test each of them on their customers. Even if the budget is too limited to afford outside assistance, there is still much that you can do yourself.

In doing so there are two major traps to be avoided:

1. Either because of incorrect market research, or an unwillingness to recognise market realities, the product is improperly positioned. This undermines the credibility, with buyers and ultimate consumers, of both what is being offered and your organisation.

2. The positioning statement decided on lacks relevance to the consumer. It may be correct, but does not excite customer interest. This is something that must be watched with particular care when entering a market for the first time.

Also, your positioning statement will involve making certain claims, actual or implied, regarding the level of service to be offered, as well as promotional support. It is important to ensure that it is possible to honour these in practice, particularly where a market some distance from Head Office, and perhaps not under your direct day-to-day control, may be involved.

One positioning plan for Europe

As pointed out above, various positioning concepts should be developed and tested. This should reveal several which could work well in all your major markets, actual or potential. Although different product benefits may have to be stressed in different markets it would clearly be beneficial if the same positioning strategy could be used in all the European markets it is planned to tackle in due course. The situation may of course exist where your product is aimed at the mass market at home but will be a niche product in all others. In such a case, and despite the disadvantages, it will be important to develop two positioning strategies. If different positioning strategies are used, you will similarly have to use varying marketing approaches in order to maintain credibility. This creates a number of practical disadvantages, absorbs more management time and creates additional cost. A single positioning strategy is the key to a standardised, integrated and effective EuroMarketing approach.

Testing it

The final shortlist of positioning statements will also require testing. This necessitates having further interviews with customers or end-users.

Other aspects you may want to research are:

- brand or product images, especially weaknesses displayed by the competition;
- buying motivations, barriers to change and how to overcome them;
- customer attitudes and profiles.

Market research agencies and some management consulting organisations are active in this sector of European research. For this more sophisticated research it is probably advisable to consider using such professional organisations, but do examine their findings critically. On occasion conclusions may be reached which your experience will make you feel are suspect. If so make this clear and demand that the conclusions be rechecked.

Positioning and the marketing mix

The positioning decided on should be reflected in the product, how it is packaged, the pricing, how it is distributed and where, and how it is promoted. In order to ensure this:

1. Talk to others in the same trade where possible. Speak with other European buyers visiting your country, attend trade fairs, take an interest in the information coming from your trade association, etc.

2. Collect information about your competitors (their brochures and articles written about them – trade fairs are a wonderful opportunity for doing this, as are friendly buyers). Observe what they are doing across Europe. Collect information from the media about them and collate it in an organised fashion so that it is readily accessible.

3. Know the most profitable groups of customers for your product/service and why this should be. In doing so take account of any market developments which could alter the present situation.

All this is going to involve the expenditure of time and effort by someone. In order to avoid waste and needless expense:

1. Pre-plan how any research is to be carried out. Who will do it, where, how long will it take, roughly how much will it cost?

2. Be clear about your research objectives. What is likely to be the commercial value of the information you are collecting? How will you use it? Is all of it essential?
3. Try to ensure your positioning concepts are linked to the product and are relevant to the consumer even before field testing is undertaken. This will avoid the expense of having to repeat the exercise, possibly on a number of occasions.
4. For anything other than straightforward desk research, the positive and negative aspects of using an outside contractor, who is trained in collecting and analysing European research, should be considered.
5. If selecting a research agency check its knowledge of your business sector, its technical capacity and its experience. This sounds obvious, but is vital, and is not always carried out effectively. Do interview more than one firm. It takes time but in choosing an organisation to carry out this research you are making a decision which could be a crucial factor in the success or failure of the EuroMarketing exercise.
6. When working with an agency, ensure that there is a clear allocation of tasks and they are given a precise written brief.
7. Take care when working in a language other than your own. Misunderstandings can and will occur unless you are an absolute expert in the language concerned. In any case reports should, wherever possible, be in your own language, otherwise not all your staff who need to are likely to be able to understand them.

Kerrygold – success in a difficult situation

'Kerrygold' is a premium-priced brand of butter marketed by the Irish Dairy Board in many European markets. Its positioning was central to the whole marketing policy and there was a particular problem in how to communicate its distinctiveness.

After developing the name, 'Kerrygold', the question was how to distinguish it from the competition, much of it produced much nearer to the point of final consumption. The product was natural, fresh, and unadulterated, but so was all butter! The product spread, and was appetising and nutritious, but that applied to all butter! The product was Irish, but heavily leaning on this one exclusive prop might cause the brand to collapse in the face of negative attitudes towards things Irish which had been revealed by research. The Irishness of the product, therefore, had to be made not only exclusive but also desirable. The concept of 'farm freshness' was selected as an additional selling point for Kerrygold, resulting in the following product positioning:

> Ireland is the emerald isle with the greenest pastures on which the finest dairy herds graze. Their milk is taken each morning to the local village creamery where it is churned that same day into butter. Irish Creamery Butter, and it's called Kerrygold, the butter that's pure village churned.

This may not seem very original, but taken in conjunction with a distinctive green and gold foil packaging (Irishness/quality), what had previously been a commodity product was transformed into a premium brand. While there was obviously advertising and promotional activity, this had to be accommodated within a relatively limited budget.

This could not have been effectively deployed without correct product positioning, which built on the positive perceptions of Irish farm produce in the minds of both buyers and end-consumers. This demonstrates that it is meeting perceptions that is important, rather than to try to find a strikingly different message, which may, as in this case, be impossible. You are looking for profitable sales, not marketing awards, always bearing in mind that the products most vulnerable to competition are those with neither a clear indication of origin or a firm identity.

To do

Now is the time to try to draft a positioning statement for your product. First, think about the four points below. They form the basic elements of a positioning strategy:

- *Target:* (the target market)

_____

_____

_____

_____

Positioning

- *Product benefit:* (direct benefit to the customer)

  _____
  _____
  _____
  _____

- *Delivery:* (what additional benefits it brings to the consumer in terms of meeting needs – could be emotional rather than substantive)

  _____
  _____
  _____
  _____

- *Origin:* (where it comes from)

- How would you characterise your product identity in these terms? What priority would you give these factors? To what degree? Do your other managers see it the same way? How do you think your existing customers would answer? Perhaps you should ask one or two with whom you are particularly friendly. Set out the results and conclusions reached.

  _____
  _____
  _____
  _____

Now, rethink the distinctiveness of your product versus your competition in the markets you intend to target. Can you think of new ways of distinguishing your product/service from the competition – particularly bearing in mind any differences in customer attitudes/perceived needs you have been able to identify?

EuroMarketing

In each case remember the Kerrygold example:

- *Product benefit:* freshness.
- *Delivery:* creaminess.
- *Origin:* Irish.

_____

_____

_____

_____

_____

Your positioning statement for Europe

Enter your ideas, and those of your colleagues, on this page. The objective is to arrive at a number of potentially feasible alternatives that can be tested with trade buyers, and consumer panels where relevant, in both existing and new potential markets. This exercise will also provide a yardstick against which to measure the findings of any outside research consultants, should these be used.

_____

_____

_____

_____

_____

CHAPTER 7

PRODUCT POLICY

Having determined the ideal positioning for your product or service it is now necessary to see what adaptations will be required to match this, but before starting this process it might be valuable to look at one example of the successful application of a standardised product development policy.

Diekirch: the quality taste for Europe

Now, I really think we are ready for the European Single Market

thought Edgar Pêcheur, Marketing Director of the Diekirch Brewery, based in the Grand Duchy of Luxembourg, right in the heart of the European Community. Pêcheur had just come back from a reception to celebrate the opening of a new bottling plant capable of turning out 46,000 bottles an hour.

The opening of the plant was the final step in a long process during which the company had reviewed its portfolio of products and its organisational structure. It wanted to be ready for the opening of the new European market. Pêcheur realised that to turn investment into profit in the Single Market his company would have to manoeuvre very carefully, as well as have the production capacity and the marketing strategy required to make Diekirch one of the top breweries in Europe.

But how did Diekirch plan to cope with the market changes taking place in Europe?

Changing beer consumption trends in Europe

Keen observation of Europe's drinking habits is a preoccupation with Diekirch as it has to anticipate consumer and industry trends in order to stay competitive. Although enjoying beer is a universal European habit, there has been a stagnation, even a decline in per capita consumption over the last few years in countries with a traditionally high consumption of beer such as Belgium, Denmark and Germany; The Netherlands being the exception. In the case of Belgium and Luxembourg, Diekirch's two biggest markets, per capita consumption has seriously decreased over the last 25 years. In contrast, bottled water and soft drinks (fruit drinks) have become more popular, with a rate of growth of 9.5 per cent and the consumption of wine has more than doubled in 25 years. In Southern Europe (Spain, Portugal, Italy and Greece), however, beer drinking is on the increase.

The pattern of consumption of the different varieties of beer has also changed, with special beers becoming more important. Beer in the Benelux is usually divided into seven different categories: pils, Trappist (named after an order of monks but brewed industrially), gueuze or acid, special beer, abbey (brewed by monks), table beers and low alcohol or alcohol-free beers.

During the 1980s, the consumption of pils as well as table beer and gueuze went down, while special beers and abbey beers grew in popularity. Also, two new beer varieties came on to the market: low alcohol and alcohol-free beers.

Consumer behaviour

The behaviour of beer drinkers has changed considerably and it is highly probable that these trends will continue. Between 1983 and 1991, the distribution of beer in barrels grew by 10 per cent, suggesting that there was greater beer consumption away from home in hotels, restaurants, cafes and bars (known as the hotel, restaurant and catering, or HORECA, sector). Furthermore, in the same period, there was a 10 per cent reduction in sales in bottles carrying deposits.

Changing patterns of distribution

Beer reaches the consumer via three separate channels: retail stores, the HORECA establishments and home delivery, some distributors being engaged in all three.

Product Policy

Direct door-to-door deliveries have become rare because of the expense. In 1960, 95 per cent of beer for household consumption was delivered directly to the home. This was down to 20 per cent by 1983 and has continued to decline to only 5 per cent. Food retailers now account for one-third of total sales volume.

Adapting the product range

In adapting to these changes Diekirch's answer was to concentrate on market niches and segments which had been neglected or ill-served by the competition. It focused on premium beers and developed special brands as part of its product portfolio which includes:

- Light, a pale flavoured ale with less alcohol content.
- Premium, a pale, light ale brewed according to the Pilsen tradition.
- Exclusive, a pale malt ale, mellow and tasty.
- Grande Reserve, a special beer brewed from selected malt, stronger and amber in colour.

The best selling brand is Premium, which on its own represents 90 per cent of current production. Edgar Pêcheur describes the positioning sought for these brands :

> We have positioned Premium at a higher level. We have tried to differentiate it from other Pils on the market by describing it as a Pils deluxe. In the segment of the deluxe ale, we developed another product, Exclusive, more malty, richer flavoured, yet mellow. Finally, Grande Reserve is an amber beer. This is the top of the mark(line).

Communication policy

One of Diekirch's objectives is to reinforce its image as a regional producer of quality beer. This is why packaging for the three new products (Premium, Exclusive and Grande Reserve) reflects the company's base in the Grand Duchy of Luxembourg, both on the label and the cap seals.

Conclusions

In comparison with the majority of businesses Diekirch is a large organisation and its approach to product policy may seem to have only limited relevance. In practice this is incorrect. Ten years ago Diekirch was only the third-ranking brand in a market of 350,000 inhabitants, albeit with a quality image. Also, the new geographical markets they have been targeting had already been penetrated by the large multinational brewers, who were able to advertise and promote their brands on a scale not open to Diekirch.

The above case study is therefore important because it shows how an independent regional producer in a mature market and with strong competition from much larger groups, was able to develop a distinct product policy. It will be noted that this was based on the identification of niche markets, followed by the use of established technical skills to produce premium quality products in order to satisfy those markets. Beers in Luxembourg are brewed to German standards of purity, which also helped to enhance the image of quality. The development of four products rather than one possessed a number of marketing advantages in that buyers could be presented with a coherent range to fill a particular market need, and consumers could vary their purchases without having to switch brands. Whether the fact that one product line accounts for 90 per cent of sales is a cause for celebration or concern only time will tell. Most firms would probably not consider this an ideal situation.

Case study – Mobalpa

Pocket-size multinational captures the European market

What sort of people are prepared to spend money on the fitted kitchen of their dreams? Finding the answer to this question has been essential for the marketing strategy of the French company, Mobalpa, which specialises in making high quality, integrated kitchen furniture. Popular taste in kitchens and kitchen furniture has changed radically in recent years and so has the way they are marketed: the ready-made kitchen unit has arrived and is here to stay. Today's kitchen is well designed, rational, simple to use, easy to clean and pleasant to live in. It has become a special place where friends and family are welcome.

The key to success: strategic focus

It took Mobalpa 30 years to become one of the top ten manufacturers of integrated kitchens in Europe. It is the market leader in France and its turnover, in 1992, reached 69 million ECU. One-third of this total comes from exports to other European countries. How has this growth been achieved? The managers of Mobalpa sum it up like this: you need a clear, concise strategy and operational efficiency.

Mobalpa's strategic formula

The company's strong performance is the result of the application of a formula made up of two essential elements:

1. It chose a specific market in which to operate, resisting the temptation to spread resources too thin, too fast.
2. The managers have taken a common-sense approach, resolving that they must concentrate on a specific niche market and, within that market, that they must lead the field.

Nationally, their customer profile is that of a middle manager or employee, aged 40 or older, who owns his or her house or apartment. He or she wants good quality products and reliable service.

Mobalpa's business concept is summed up in the phrase: 'Mobalpa is everyday comfort'. Mobalpa makes sure that it meets these demands for quality and service. It also manages to make the kitchen units so that the basic framework can be standardised but the appearance changed to meet the needs and tastes of each customer.

'Do it better, do more.'

This ambition, stated by the company, is not just another advertising phrase, but rather the expression of a determination to keep moving towards excellence. In 1992 Mobalpa won the Grand Prix de la Qualité given by the Association Française pour la Qualité Totale de l'Ameublement. Its reputation for quality is a company asset when marketing its products. It also boasts reliable customer service, low production costs and high profits. That is the ideal strategic situation every business must seek.

Market fragmentation and the European dimension

At Mobalpa, there is no product specifically designed for a national market. All products are offered and available throughout Europe. However, the company takes advantage of cultural differences between Europeans to expand the scope of its products beyond its already wide range. This is how successful models in France originated from Belgium and Great Britain, and vice versa.

The managers of Mobalpa emphasise that access to a European market is a natural progression for them and it helps to bring in new ideas and generate different questions to which they must find the answers. While exploiting European differences and offering a wide range of products to satisfy the personal tastes of every European, Mobalpa has become the only trade name in its field with a truly European dimension, while avoiding sacrificing the French reputation for stylish design in the process.

EuroMarketing: a reality for Mobalpa

It is possible for Mobalpa to sell the same product in every country throughout the EC, although there are no European standards for fitted kitchens. The company is, in fact, part of a group working to establish such standards.

In terms of Mobalpa's pricing policy, all countries are treated in the same way. The company feels that, whatever the country, each retailer ought to be able to obtain the same gross margin, before deduction of sales operating expenses. Through this type of equality, Mobalpa has managed to win loyalty from those to whom it links its destiny.

In the area of sales promotions, after an attempt to use a visual message and an approach specific to each country failed, the company turned to national professionals better skilled at making specific adaptations. They have to operate within the context that Mobalpa's brand name and dedication to quality must be mentioned in all promotions.

A system of incentives has been designed for retailers, offering them an advertising participation bonus at the end of the year and a contribution from Mobalpa to local marketing expenditures. Conversely, a contribution to general marketing overheads (for a national television advertising campaign for example) is required of the retailer.

Conclusions

The Mobalpa story clearly illustrates a number of points. First, the necessity of taking a long-term view, markets are not developed successfully overnight, it normally takes time to build up a significant presence.

Product Policy

Second, the concentration on a specific niche within their field. Third, the clear identification of a target group of customers. Their concentration on quality should also be noted. Putting in place good quality control systems, based on the concepts contained in the ISO 9000 standard, cuts wastage, reduces costs and allows the delivery of a product of consistent quality. Nothing is better designed to promote confidence, both among trade dealers and the buying public. This is essential when seeking to establish a reputation in a new market, and at the same time achieve a realistic margin on sales.

Remaining barriers to product standardisation

Relatively early on you will have made an analysis of the legal and administrative barriers to the European wide standardisation of your products and services. Now is the time to resurrect this data, and to couple it with your other market research in order to evaluate the relative importance of all the barriers identified. It is suggested you do this separately for every product or service you would like to market in another European country, so that you can summarise for each the reasons why standardisation would be either impossible or inadvisable. Some factors worth considering are:

- different consumer expectations;
- national technical standards required;
- special requirements of those you need to sell your product or service (for example packaging);
- legal restrictions;
- logistical requirements (frequency and speed of delivery, 'just in time', quantities required per delivery);
- different product positioning;
- language requirements and existing degree of understanding of the product.

You will also have to consider other factors peculiar to your own situation. You should always bear in mind that total standardisation is only worthwhile if it saves costs, improves margins and leads to more sales. It is not

EuroMarketing

an end in itself and there may well be occasions where, for perfectly good reasons, only partial standardisation, or no standardisation at all, is the correct answer. Some advice as to how to proceed with this exercise follows.

Do not forget also to compare your proposed solutions with what your present and future competitors have done. You can always learn from their successes and failures.

Ask yourself – product development

- In which European markets, whether or not served currently, do you think you could sell one or more of your current products or services without any changes of significance and still be in accord with the positioning statement you have developed?

    For convenience it is suggested you list them in the manner set out below:

    Name of the product:
    Countries where complete standardisation possible:

    Countries where only minor changes required:
    Country   Change required   Reasons

    Implications (cost/other):

    Action proposed:

Developing your EuroProduct

Researching customer requirements

The marketing function always starts with knowing who the customer is and what he or she wants. Even for high technology products, marketing is the key. If you make a technological 'winner' but have not thought about the marketing approach required, selling it successfully could be a hit and miss affair.

Really successful marketing organisations try to anticipate customer requirements; being customer driven allows them to improve existing products and develop new ones for clients which may have very different habits, tastes and cultural backgrounds. The ideal is to develop products which sell equally well to customers with similar characteristics in Greece as in Denmark, in the UK or in France.

Before asking yourself questions relating to product innovation and development do you know:

- What similar products or services to those you are contemplating providing are already on the European market?

- What your buyer and/or end-consumer would expect from your product or service?

These may sound like obvious points, repeating what has gone before, but are worth considering again in the context of product development. So many companies make the mistake of not doing so and their marketing efforts suffer as a result. Knowing the level of quality and service which potential buyers and end-users require is a good first step to approaching the European marketplace. The research which you have already undertaken should provide the answers you need.

'One-off' exercises in market research undoubtedly bring dividends, but it is also advisable to have a system where client information, including complaints, is systematically fed to your product development team. This means that your salesforce and those developing products need to talk to each other regularly in a structured fashion. Equally, top management must be intimately involved. Otherwise lessons being learned in the marketplace, including new developments by your competitors, will simply not be used to advantage.

Product specialisation

Every company has to assess its own product range, its acceptability in new markets and the competition it is likely to face. Some companies are expanding their product range so as to appeal to ever broadening buyers' requests and consumers' wants. Most successful EuroMarketing companies are not expanding their product range in this way. In fact, some are reducing it in order better to concentrate their strengths and reduce or eliminate weaknesses.

ICC, an example of an SME which has landed on its feet

The story of this SME is the story of an engineer, Teofilo Leite, who devised a project for the marketing of shoes to a highly specialised segment of the market: that for industrial footwear. To do so he created his own company, ICC, in 1988. Although shoes for industrial use represent only 3 per cent of the market, this niche market, in his view, was easier to penetrate and, most importantly, easier to internationalise.

The brand adopted was Lavaro and the positioning encapsulated a highly creative slogan 'Job Fitted Shoes'. Unlike traditional products in this field however, from the very beginning ICC combined a fashion design component with the inevitable requirement of providing protection for the wearer. In addition, a standard range of products at the same price, is offered to all existing markets. These include most of the EU and remaining EFTA countries.

According to Mr Teofilo Leite, the decision to specialise in a niche market was the major reason for the success of his business:

> When we first started we produced both work shoes and fashion shoes. Since we have concentrated more exclusively on the Lavaro brand of industrial footwear the company has grown. Specialisation in a specific area is the only way for a small business like ours to avoid having to compete on prices with the large scale manufacturers, and in particular with countries that can combine low labour costs with raw materials such as South America or the Indian sub-continent.

This example illustrates how specialising in one particular area with a rationalising product range can be an efficient way for an SME to focus resources, which in turn enables them to afford the marketing activity necessary to seize new opportunities. When selling to other markets an element of range rationalisation will be almost inevitable. Very few firms will be able to market their whole product line successfully in another country and an attempt to do so introduces complexities and can be counter-productive. It is wise to remember the rule that 80 per cent of sales are derived from 20 per cent of the product range. When entering new markets it is better to concentrate sole attention on the 20 per cent and what is needed to replicate their success in existing markets.

Product quality

Choosing the right level of quality is all important. Sometimes only the best is good enough. More often what is required is a satisfactory and constant level. Your market research will indicate what is appropriate in your case, although it is important to appreciate that when tackling specialised niche markets a high level of quality is frequently required.

Like many companies you are probably grappling with the issue of quality and how you can demonstrate it to your customers. This is something that is too important to be left to chance, requiring the development of a systematic approach. In order to consider what is right in the context of your business it is suggested you address the following questions:

- Do you see your product as offering high quality/medium quality/low quality?
- Do your managers agree?
- Is the question of quality ever formally discussed at meetings within the company?
- Are the results of discussions on quality regularly on the agenda of meetings of the board of directors?
    - How do you define quality in relation to your product?
    - Do your managers and salesforce have the same definition?
    - Do you know what your customers require in terms of quality?
    - How do they define quality?
    - To what extent does your product match with these requirements?
    - Do you offer any warranty or guarantee on the product or service?
    - If not, would this provide an additional and quantifiable marketing advantage at an acceptable cost?
    - How do you ensure you maintain the desired level of quality in a consistent fashion?
    - Do you know about EN 29000/ISO 9000 series of Quality Assurance standards?
    - Have you thought about what might be involved in achieving

formal certification to the applicable part of that series of standards and the result in terms of costs and benefits?
- Even if certification is inappropriate would it nevertheless be advisable to adopt the underlying principles within your organisation?
- Have you ever thought of applying the concept of total quality management (TQM)?

We can only repeat the advice to find out from your customers the level of quality they want and for which they are prepared to pay. This can reduce the number and gravity of mistakes made in the field of product development. Finally, be ruthless when deciding which products should or should not be brought to the market. Remember that only a small minority out of those introduced ever find a significant long-term place in the market.

European technical product standards

As we have seen, differences in technical requirements throughout the EU constitute one of the most significant barriers to trade remaining within the Single Market. If technical product standards affect you, then there are several questions you should be asking:

- Are the national standards to which you are currently conforming accepted without the need for further testing in the new markets you are targeting?
- Are you aware of European standards that might apply to your product range?
- If so, are you aware of the required testing and certification procedures, as well as the mandatory use of the CE Marking for certain products?

Technical product standardisation is a complex area and it is impossible to explain adequately within a guide of this nature. It is strongly advised that you contact your national standards body in order to receive help in answering the above questions and to gather other relevant information, not least that concerning quality assurance certification (frequently very important if you are considering bidding for public contracts). Please remember that if some of your products are imported into the EU they will still have to meet the same requirements as those produced locally, and the legal liability will be yours if this is not done.

Looking for similarities

It is important to remember that successful EuroMarketers do not simply make a good product and sell it across Europe. They investigate what it will take to make a product for the European market. Sometimes it requires very little in the way of modification to make a EuroProduct, like Illycaffe's Italian Espresso. For other products, it will be harder. Among considerations to be taken into account when developing such a product will include whether your European customers use your products in the same way, whether similarities can be found in terms of customer requirements, and if there are any technical differences which need to be overcome.

It is important to utilise any existing experience you may have. For example, if you have sold your product(s) in another country, have you ever had to change and adapt it/them to that market? If so, what was the reason? Is this equally valid in relation to the present exercise?

Research you have conducted in several European markets has possibly led you to find certain similarities, together with ways in which a new product can be adapted in order to become a EuroProduct. In addition, if you are currently making bespoke or 'made to order' products, have you thought about developing your own design based on the experience gained and selling that?

To sum up

You should by now have identified all the barriers to standardising those products or services you hope to market in other countries, setting these out in an easily usable format. What you now have to do is to determine the instances where standardisation would pay, and to what extent it should be carried out.

In doing this it is important to be realistic. The Single Market is still in its early days. At this stage it is very possible that you will need to compromise, dividing Europe in two or three regions, choosing to attack first those countries with enough common features to allow for the effective marketing of a standard product.

This is a difficult process requiring creative thinking. However, the rewards in terms of making your business more focused and efficient, as well as in other cost savings that should result, could be substantial. Nevertheless, do not be carried away by excessive enthusiasm. Always remember that any changes you make must have the whole-hearted support of

Product Policy

your existing distribution channels and be seen as an improvement by end-users. If you do not you could threaten the existing foundations of your company's prosperity.

So, briefly set down the changes you intend to make on the next page, consider them carefully, and test them on your customer base before taking any irrevocable action.

EuroMarketing

Product adaptations for the European Market

CHAPTER 8

PRICING POLICY

Pricing

Managers throughout Europe are unanimous on one point: setting the right price is one of the most difficult tasks of marketing a product. In doing so there are a variety of considerations to be taken into account, quite apart from technical factors such as required rates of return and whether you should use the marginal or full recovery methods of product costing. This is a subject to be discussed with your financial advisers as it is important to appreciate that this book only seeks to deal with the marketing aspect of product pricing.

Premium pricing

While every company's marketing mix is different, successful EuroMarketers like Mobalpa and Illycaffe charge premium prices for their high quality products and are not afraid to do so. In the case of Illycaffe, the pricing policy of this espresso producer is based on the quality and service it offers to its customers; its personal relations with the bar operators; the ability to guarantee profits; the supply of collateral services such as espresso machines and cups for the bar; and, the provision of financing and discounts.

While most competitors focus on the discounts, Illy emphasises good relations and profits. But it does not try to raise the profits of clients by lowering their costs. In fact, Illy charges up to twice as much for its coffee as its next leading competitor. Its policy is to raise profits by increasing consumption. As Riccardo Illy describes it:

Clients that claim they are unable to afford the high price of Illycaffe are offered the opportunity to try the coffee for six months. During that time, the operator is asked to register the number of cups of espresso coffee consumed each day. At the end of the trial period, most bar owners are already convinced of the advantages of serving Illy coffee. For those who are not yet sure, it is enough to sit down with them and calculate the increase in consumption and the overall increase in profits since they began serving Illycaffe. Every time this calculation is positive, we've gained a new client. When it is negative, we promise to reimburse all of the costs of the trial period plus the promised increase in profit. In ten years of operating under this policy, we have only had to reimburse one client.

Price and quality

The premium price/quality relationship is a key factor to most if not all successful EuroMarketers.

The pricing policy of a manufacturer of natural flavourings, Perlarom, depends on a variety of factors including the client's industrial area and individual needs. It is customary in the flavour industry for invitations to bid for a contract to be sent to several companies. Customers try to obtain significant discounts, knowing of the high margins which traditionally exist in the flavour industry. Perlarom's managers are not worried about price competition because they offer high quality products. Even competitors offering prices which are up to 30 per cent lower are unsuccessful in capturing their customers because of the high quality of the total package which they offer, resulting in better value for money.

SMEs in the US

In the US, SMEs with a coast-to-coast marketing strategy use premium pricing as a strategic weapon. It is unlikely to be a coincidence that successful SMEs on both sides of the Atlantic use the same strategy.

In researching US SMEs it is clear that under-pricing is a common mistake of those companies that are not successful. Pricing at the high end of the pricing options is a common feature of those that are, for the following reasons:

1. A key part of high pricing is to ensure that the marketing programme is able to provide enhanced value in terms of the customers' percep-

Pricing Policy

tions. This may include features such as guarantees, a high level of sales support and excellent service.
2. If the price is too low the company does not have the margin and financial resources to implement its plan to launch its product or service in new markets.
3. It is much easier to lower prices later, either directly or through discounts, than to raise prices.
4. Having enough margin allows the company to give higher rates of return to intermediaries involved in product distribution, which is another common element in these success cases.
5. Having enough margin allows the company to spend more on advertising and promotion than the competition during the national expansion (roll-out).
6. Having enough margin allows the company to pay for the growth of the company's internal overheads arising from servicing more customers and higher stock levels.

A single pricing policy

There are good reasons why companies like Pie Medical have switched to a single pricing policy for their European markets. Without one they are more susceptible when negotiating separate contract terms with different clients to acceding to pressure for lower prices, particularly where customers suspect pricing differences exist. Moreover, each local distribution organisation can use its bargaining power to obtain the lowest price possible, therefore disrupting the product positioning on some markets.

Pie's product is now sold across Europe and to the US for the same transfer price. Pie Medical experimented in the past with a quantity discount price policy based on cumulative sales. The discount strategy aimed to increase sales by giving financial incentives. A higher number of units were actually sold, but net margins decreased.

Re-imports and parallel imports

For products easily transportable across Europe, another basic problem of not having a common pricing strategy is the danger of stimulating parallel imports. The more packaging is standardised and multilanguage labelling is used, the more attractive this operation becomes, always supposing the product is well enough established in a market, and a sufficiently wide price anomaly exists to allow purchases to be made at the wholesale level in another country.

Parallel importing can be made more difficult through a single-language labelling policy, although it would certainly raise manufacturing and warehousing costs due to the small lot-sizes – and there are multilingual countries like Belgium where this obviously would not work.

One way they should not be controlled is through including unduly restrictive clauses in sales agreements. These are always in danger of being regarded as illegal under European competition law and should be avoided. The best solution is to bring prices across Europe in line to an extent which makes parallel importing unprofitable.

There remains the problem of convincing those distributing the product in another market, unless they are under your direct control, of the importance of maintaining price and discount discipline. How you will achieve this in practice deserves considerable thought seeing this will have to be achieved without the threat of sanctions. In practice, the best way of achieving this is to offer such an attractive overall package that distributors realise that it is against their own interest to break ranks and depart from agreed pricing and discount structures.

In the light of the points made in this section, please address the questions which follow on the next page.

Pricing Policy

Things To do

As has been seen pricing is a complex issue which involves more than positioning alone. Pricing, after all, is directly linked to the profitability of your company and this must never be forgotten.

Within the framework of this book we can only draw your attention to the need for:

- pricing consistent with your EuroMarketing positioning statement;
- consistent pricing throughout the EC.

The questions to resolve, therefore are:

- What pricing policy is consistent with the positioning statement and with the required sales margin?

  _____
  _____
  _____
  _____
  _____

- Can this price be applied throughout the EC?

  _____
  _____
  _____
  _____

- If so, are there any ways, without distorting your operations, in which you could restructure in order to make unitary pricing possible?

  _____
  _____
  _____
  _____

EuroMarketing

- If not, would it be possible to at least harmonise pricing in some markets, particularly those that border on one another?

  _____
  _____
  _____
  _____

- Should possible currency fluctuations be a problem in achieving unitary pricing have you considered the advantages of purchasing foreign exchange cover in order to bring greater certainty to your calculations? Or, if you are selling to a country with a strong and stable currency, taking out loans in that currency to the extent they will be matched by eventual receipts?

  _____
  _____
  _____
  _____

- Having taken all factors into account, what will be your pricing policy in Europe?

  _____
  _____
  _____
  _____

- Do not forget also to compare **your** pricing policy with that of present and future competitors.

  _____
  _____

Pricing Policy

CHAPTER 9

SALES AND DISTRIBUTION POLICY

Sales and distribution

Establishing satisfactory arrangements for sales and distribution in another market is difficult for the smaller company, particularly when their product and service is completely unknown and the resources that are available for promotional activity are limited.

In markets where there are never going to be more than a small number of direct purchasers, and substantial media advertising and other promotional activities are unlikely to be required, then direct control by an existing sales executive is feasible. This, however, will not be a satisfactory solution in the majority of instances, particularly when any element of after-sales service is involved. In addition, it is difficult to keep abreast of market changes from a distance.

The establishment of a subsidiary company or branch can be considered, but its oversight and control will constitute an additional burden for existing management. Unless they have the time available this can be a dangerous undertaking. In any case, the subsidiary operation will need to be run by someone with experience of the market. Should you lack someone in your team with the required knowledge, whose services you can spare for an indefinite period, it will obviously be necessary to recruit and train someone from the country concerned.

Before taking this step, even if it makes good commercial sense, and there are advantages in being able to wholly control the launch of a mar-

Sales and Distribution Policy

keting operation in another country, it is essential to take legal advice. There will almost certainly be a number of consequential legal obligations with which you will be unfamiliar, not only to the State but to any employee engaged. For example, problems arise in some countries if you use the services of someone full-time but on a self-employed basis. In such circumstances the revenue service may classify the person as being a full-time employee and regard your company as *de facto* operating and established in the country. The result could be your being responsible for the payment of quite substantial employer social security contributions.

An alternative course, pursued by the majority of smaller companies, is to either appoint a sole agent, who books orders for you to invoice and deliver, or a distributor who both sells and physically distributes. The problem is to find the right one, particularly in view of the EU legislation covering the rights of sales agents. Termination of a contract with either a sole agent or distributor can render you liable to pay significant sums in compensation.

While finding an organisation whose capacity you trust and which you can work with co-operatively is essential, a major problem exists. Even the most competent agent or distributor can only concentrate attention on the products of a limited number of principals. If they are well established they are likely to already have a considerable number for whom they act. The question you have to decide is how you can make your offer sufficiently attractive to make them be prepared to work hard for you, not only during the launch phase, which most will do, but thereafter.

Do also remember, and this is important in terms of establishing pricing structures, that the days when distributors were prepared to buy at a price and then take responsibility for all the promotional and advertising costs, have largely gone. Nowadays the attitude normally taken by a distributor is that it is your brand they are selling, and it is you who will gain most long-term value from their efforts. Thus you should be prepared to participate to a significant extent in meeting the advertising and promotional costs. Preferably, providing you can afford it and have confidence in being able to establish yourself on the market, this should not be in the form of a percentage rebate on sales, but as an agreed contribution, to be decided annually. In any case, your making a concrete contribution to the selling effort, including the training of the distributor's team, is going to be one of the keys to success. The difficult decision to be taken is how much money you are prepared to risk in advance of knowing what volume of sales is likely to result.

If you do decide the most appropriate action is to appoint an agent or distributor, and before doing so you need to have worked out the details of the offer you will make, how do you go about finding one? A variety of methods exist:

- using the services of your national export promotional organisation;
- utilising any links your chamber of commerce may have with the market concerned;
- seeking a partner through the European Commission's Business Cooperation Network (your nearest European Information Centre can provide the address of the adviser nearest to you);
- going on organised trade missions;
- exhibiting at trade fairs, or just visiting and talking to appropriate exhibitors (although taking the latter course will provide you with a more restricted choice and may not be the best option);
- asking potential customers for recommendations when conducting market research, but beware, their views may be coloured by personal or other considerations. Only if the same firm is named on more than one occasion can the advice be guaranteed to be disinterested. If asking their opinion regarding a specific organisation do appreciate their natural reluctance to make critical comments to a third party. Such verbal references frequently have very little value.

Should you be prepared to consider selling someone else's product or service as well as your own there is another approach that might be considered, although the search procedure will still be the same. This is to locate a firm in the market, of similar size and outlook, which has products which you would be prepared to market in your own country, and who in return would market yours. Providing sales for both parties reach satisfactory levels such arrangements can work well and be long-lasting.

Before you make any decisions as to the type of distribution channel to use, consider some concrete examples of how others have approached this problem.

SMEs in the US

From an analysis of the firms interviewed in the US it is clear that a key success factor is not to underestimate the difficulty of the sales effort and the training required for those involved in distribution.

Sales and Distribution Policy

Many successful American companies go one step further, however, in that they challenge the normal distribution concepts and experiment with other ways of getting the product to the consumer. They start by asking themselves a number of questions. These include:

- What is the full cost of using the established and normal channel? When the pricing, cost and margin analysis indicate that the normal channel is too costly for the benefit provided, the company experiments with a new approach.
- What value in terms of product/service support is being provided by the established channel and is it satisfactory? This is a particularly important question for new products that require the training of sales personnel or extra introductory efforts.
- Is there a new type of distribution channel that has developed since the industry leaders developed their marketing approach?

Some specific examples follow of how American SMEs have organised their distribution network by looking for alternative distribution channels, or used distinctive promotional methods in order to utilise existing channels better.

Monster Cable

Monster Cable was created by one man who had been a manufacturers' representative to the audio industry calling on audio retailers. He designed a new speaker cable and began selling it himself in his own territory. He soon learned that retailers are sceptical about buying new products because they want guaranteed sales and profits.

Keeping this in mind, he developed a sales and distribution strategy that included a display rack and packaging which explained the advantages of Monster Cable. The pricing strategy provided good profits to the retailer and he set up a training and follow-up programme for the retail sales assistants. He also obtained permission from retailers to put up charts which prominently displayed the performance of individual sales personnel. His sales representatives then worked with those sales people who sold the lowest amount of Monster Cable in order to improve their performance. This helped the retailers by providing sales training to their staff and increased the sales of Monster Cable by ensuring that all sales people knew how to sell it. Once the system was established, representatives were recruited to cover the entire country. The roll-out was supported by only limited advertising, but an extensive public relations campaign, coupled with the organisation of product testing by writers for specialised audio magazines.

Tripledge

Tripledge windscreen wipers were originally sold through normal retail outlets (auto parts supply stores) in the region where the company was based. In determining how to go national the company president decided that, using traditional sales outlets, he would need US$10 million up front and the company would have to advertise prior to getting distribution in most markets. This was because retailers would be unwilling to take on the product in this competitive category without seeing advertising first. They would also require the retail price to be set at US$9.95 since that was the standard set by competition. Most retailers would not carry every size but only those that sold best.

This was clearly an unattractive situation and warranted consideration of the taking of a different selling approach. Tripledge determined that, since some special order sizes were sold for as much as US$49.95, and no competitor provided a life of the car guarantee, they could, providing they offered this assurance, double their price for all sizes to US$19.95 and still be perceived as giving value to the end-consumer. Setting the higher price also permitted them to experiment with a direct marketing strategy. They sold the wipers direct through inserts mailed with credit card statements and in catalogues. They also used the print media and TV advertising. They got on to TV by paying 40 per cent commission on sales to specialised companies that did both the advertising and direct selling on their behalf. This eliminated all up-front charges and advertising risk to Tripledge. Through the use of this overall policy Tripledge now has national coverage and has exceeded its original sales goals for the national roll-out.

Dell computer company

Dell began selling personal computers assembled from components which the founder of the company had in his garage. This man realised that successful sales of personal computers relied on the following factors:
1. The machine be designed in such a way as to enable its assembly to fit the exact need of the purchaser. There are literally thousands of

Sales and Distribution Policy

potential combinations of memory size, cache size, hard disk size and speed, floppy disk size and speed, video type, input/output options, case configuration, add-in boards, etc, which could be asked for.

2. Providing excellent customer service and a full guarantee.
3. Fast delivery of the exact computer desired.
4. Perceived value for money.

Although Dell's success is judged in the media to be the result of low pricing, his computers have never been the cheapest on the market. There have always been other directly marketed computers available at lower prices. Dell, however, by pricing at close to normal retail prices, built in enough margin to not only provide a good product but also excellent customer service. Other direct marketers selling solely on price have continuously received poor publicity because of service problems.

Dell became the largest and fastest growing personal computer manufacturer by building a direct response system that focused on assembling the unit to order, shipping within one week and, most importantly, providing the best guarantee and service in the industry. The sales catalogue and follow-up mailings to both existing customers and enquirers are of a high standard. For several years Dell has been the top-rated computer company in the US for providing customer service and satisfaction.

In addition, there is an example of how a European firm has addressed the problem of achieving distribution.

Preveza

For many years Greece has been a major exporter of textiles. Greek companies have taken advantage of cheap labour costs to produce low-priced, good quality products which are attractive to buyers in other countries. Recognising this potential from a very early date, the Argyros family, the main shareholder in Preveza, became involved in the textiles business. They owned and managed a number of factories in Athens as well as in other areas of Greece and began exporting in the late 1940s. During the 1960s the group of companies expanded rapidly and in 1977 a new factory was opened, near the city of Preveza, about 400kms north-west of Athens and close to the port of Igoumenitsa.

Initially, the export drive of Preveza was based mainly on the relative cheapness of its product. Greek manufacturers have a price and quality advantage over their EC competitors due to the excellent quality of cotton

EuroMarketing

which is grown in their country and a plentiful supply of cheap, local labour. As international conditions have changed, in particular with low priced competition from Asian countries, Preveza has altered its marketing strategy away from competing on price. The emphasis is now on quality, customer services and support.

Preveza sells its product through a network of agents. For each EU country one agent is employed on an exclusive basis, with the exception of France and Germany where two agents are used. The agents are small, highly specialised firms, which employ from two to seven people. They usually represent a significant number of textile producers from around the world. For each successful sale they receive a commission of 2–3 per cent of the total sales value.

The agents are carefully chosen. Customers may recommend them or word may get round that this particular firm is effective. Once appointed they are assessed once a year or every two years. There are two key evaluation criteria: total sales for their area or country and whether the agent's customers have payments outstanding.

Once agents have been appointed they receive significant support. Important potential new customers, found by the agents, are always visited by Preveza managers prior to any order being taken. This visit serves to identify specific needs in terms of quality and service and to convince the company that Preveza can satisfy those needs. As a matter of routine, the same managers visit all customers once a year for public relations purposes and to clear up any difficulties the customers may have.

Sales and Distribution Policy

Ask yourself – in the light of the information given

- For each of the markets you are targeting, which would seem the most appropriate channel of distribution:
  - selling and delivering direct;
  - establishing a subsidiary;
  - establishing a branch;
  - utilising a national of the market concerned, but on a self-employed basis;
  - a sales agency, with you invoicing and delivering;
  - a comprehensive sales and distribution organisation;
  - a company in the same line of business on a reciprocal sales basis;
  - any other you can think of.
- Now set out the methods you will use in the search for appropriate partners.
- How will you find out whether any organisation identified is satisfactory?
- In the case of agents or distributors, can a sufficiently attractive package be assembled in order to attract one of good quality?

Try setting out the specific contract details, together with the costs involved, looking carefully for gaps and weaknesses in what is being provided. When doing so try to put yourself in the position of someone considering the offer. Remember when undertaking this exercise that you and any potential distributor will have to agree on a variety of things, such as the best way to deliver your goods or services to your customer, quantitative sales targets, standards of service, quality requirements, the length of the agreement, the promotional programme, etc.

As well as setting out what you can offer, develop some standard criteria as to what you expect from your distributors, in the form of a distribution document. This will help to achieve consistency in your distribution arrangements and, once again, help to clarify your own objectives.

Further guidance is given on the next page.

EuroMarketing

Your distribution document

Having decided on which distribution system to use, you will still have to design a complete distribution strategy and communicate this to all those persons and organisations involved in the distribution network. The best way to do this is to develop what is known as a Distribution Document.

In doing so basic questions to be answered include:

- What are the necessary steps to be taken to ensure effective distribution of your products?
- Who is responsible, or is likely to be responsible, for these operations?
- What services will have to be provided by the distribution channel?
- How, when third parties are involved, are the operations to be divided between you and others in the distribution chain?
- Who will be in charge of the promotion and merchandising of the product in the field?
- Who will be in charge of after-sales service? What will need to be provided?

Here are some points it is suggested be included in your distribution document:

- Your goals in respect of territorial coverage, actions to be taken, within what timescale, and those responsible.
- A short analysis of the current market situation as it would appear from your research.
- The development of the economic/market situation where this is likely to have a marked impact.
- A definition of the needs of clients in the selected countries – divided by type where necessary.
- Identification of the players in the distribution process.
- The main distribution networks available and their relative strengths and weaknesses in terms of ensuring your objectives are met at an acceptable cost.
- An assessment of the competition and how they may react to a new and significant entrant to the market.

- An assessment of the company's strong and weak points compared to its competition and any actions to be taken.
- The sales volumes you hope to achieve.

CHAPTER 10

PROMOTIONAL POLICY

Brand building and advertising

The actions of the Irish Dairy Board (IDB) provide a good example, although they can hardly be classified as an SME, of how a brand can successfully be introduced to new markets and finally achieve a trans-European identity. From the outset it was intended that 'Kerrygold' butter should be a standard product in most markets and this has been largely achieved. All the 'Kerrygold' butter sold in mainland European markets is of the unsalted variety, in a standard size and packaging. The gold foil wrapper is the same in all markets, except for the text which is overprinted in the appropriate languages. The brand identity may vary slightly from country to country, but the brand name and the core communication strategy are common to all markets. This has opened up opportunities for achieving economies of scale in almost every aspect of Kerrygold's marketing mix and these have been quickly recognised and exploited by the IDB.

The IDB started their marketing campaign with thorough research. The results of a consumer survey in the UK indicated that Ireland was not a particularly desirable product origin compared to other countries. Many British housewives ranked Ireland as last choice or gave it no ranking at all. On the other hand, there was a low level of awareness about Irish butter, i.e. no negative stigmas such as 'cheapness'. After a target market and distribution channel were chosen, and a brand name, packaging and price level decided on, an advertising campaign was developed. Television was the chosen medium for the launch advertising campaign. In total, media advertising accounted for 73 per cent of the marketing support budget, the rest went on selling incentives, display material, merchandising and public relations.

Standardised EuroAdvertising

Promotion had been managed on a country-by-country basis until recently. A major turning point occurred in 1990 when a pan-European advertising campaign was developed which has since been shown successfully in all the Kerrygold markets. This campaign is based on an emotional 'green' positioning which communicates an image of premium dairy products from Ireland, the land of unpolluted and unspoiled countryside. This is encapsulated in the punchline 'Pure Kerrygold from Ireland – the land that's always been green'.

The creative strategy and production of this campaign, which included both TV and press advertisements, was developed by one company. The core advertisements were then translated and adapted for each of the EU markets by local agencies affiliated with the main agency. Media planning and buying were also handled in this way.

Conclusions

While the Irish Dairy Board is a substantial operation, possessing a scale of resources not available to many businesses, one important point does stand out. Initially advertising was organised on a national basis but has progressively been integrated.

Whatever the advertising mix decided on, and this depends on the product and service and the financial resources available, any attempt at a unified approach will be nullified if you do not decide on the strategy and ensure its broad objectives are followed in every country. Naturally there will be some changes in detailed strategy to take account of differences in distribution channels, consumer preferences and culture.

What you should ask yourself – and do

Taking account of what was said in the previous section, it is necessary to look at what you are already doing successfully, the extent this could be employed in your new target markets, and any changes that will be required.

Current promotional materials
Try to assemble the promotional material you use currently:

- materials aimed at establishing corporate identity;
- sales literature;
- packaging and other designs;
- current media advertising;
- direct mail material;
- public relations literature;
- sales promotion materials.

The sort of questions you should be asking yourself include the following:

- Does your company regularly put out press releases?
- Do you undertake any formal sales promotion activity?
- Are you satisfied with your current promotional activity?
- Are you sure it meets market needs to the extent you are able to afford?
- Are there ways in which it could be improved?
- Have you ever undertaken promotional activity in another European market?
- If so, would you do it the same way, or would you make changes?

Have you ever tried talking with anyone in your trade that has undertaken some of the types of promotional activity with which you have no prior experience? They could provide lessons that you could put to practical use.

Your Competitor's Promotional Activity
This can also be a fruitful source of information and give you pointers as to how you should organise your activities. Try to assemble examples of as much of their material as you can and compare it with your own. What lessons are there to be learned?

Your customers
As part of your market research you should by now have talked to a considerable number of customers, actual and potential. What lessons did this exercise provide concerning the promotional mix they would favour?

It's your decision
Only you can set your sales targets, determine the promotional margins available, and the resulting budget for these activities. What we would suggest you do next is to decide on the appropriate allocation between direct media advertising, below-the-line activity and public relations. This will be based on a combination of your own experience, decisions taken regarding product positioning, observation of the activities of your competitors and the knowledge gained during the market research exercise.

Advertising, not least the cost of artwork and origination, and the production of other advertising material is expensive. In order to avoid waste do discuss your plans with key customers as well as prospective distributors in other markets before placing any orders. If you can show them 'mock ups' of what is intended so much the better. If possible the programme should be tested in a restricted area, where costs can be kept down and the results closely monitored.

It is likely that you will ask for help in completing this part of the guide from your advertising agents, and from the organisation conducting your public relations if you have one. One question to be asked is if they will possess the appropriate level of experience required to support your operations now that their geographical scope is going to be considerably widened. If you are uncertain it might be wise to ask for competing organisations with an appropriate experience profile to make presentations of their ideas as to what should be included in your programme and the central message to be deployed.

Choosing agencies

As has already been said, your chances of success will be enhanced if you are able to use specialised help in areas such as research, product positioning, design, advertising, public relations, sales promotion and direct mail.

For you it is essential to use an agency which is capable of designing and implementing a European market or product research programme or standardised advertising campaign. You will only be able to maximise the benefits of standardisation when working with one agency for your European market. Bear in mind, however, that most big multinational agencies do not like to work for smaller companies. You may have to convince them it is worthwhile working for you on the basis of your future prospects.

Checklist for choosing a consultancy

- Draw up a detailed and specific brief of what you require of them.
- Ask everyone who might be able to help for names of organisations which could possibly fulfil your requirements.
- Try to have at least three organisations make presentations and evaluate them according to the following criteria:
- the relevance of their European experience, substantiated by examples of recent work;
- history of the consultancy and recent track record;
- references from previous clients, preferably in your sector;
- its size in relation to the scale of the project: do these match?
- resources location, offices in Europe.

Check that proposals include

- A full response to the brief, demonstrating understanding of the issues to be tackled, and indicating how the objectives will be met.

Promotional Policy

- Details of the specific programme of work to be carried out.
- Details of the team that will work on the project (not just on the presentation), its European experience and language capabilities.
- The consultancy's terms and conditions of business.
- A clear statement of fees and costs in the currency of your choice.

When making your decision, ask yourself four questions:

- Is the chemistry right?
- Will I get an honest answer?
- Will I enjoy and feel comfortable working with them?
- Do I trust them to deliver excellent results?

When you have made your final choice, you may want to test the agency first with a relatively small assignment. Then, evaluate the agency's performance and compare the results with earlier expectations. Where possible have colleagues or partners in other countries do the same and compare those results with your own.

In order to help you in this whole process of deciding on the content and form of your future promotional activities, and to prepare briefs for outside agencies, it is necessary to look in more detail at some of the issues involved and the choices open to you.

A consistent message throughout Europe

Every company has an identity and personality. All forms of communication leave an image of your product and company with your customers. If this sounds like an obvious remark, it is not. Many companies embark on communications activities to meet specific needs without proper consideration of the broader picture.

Advertising, public relations, sales promotion cannot in isolation create an identity for a product, or raise awareness of its distinctive features, throughout Europe. Rather, the shoe is on the other foot. The Kerrygold example shows the importance of positioning to the whole communications effort, from packaging to advertising. Only when a product's identity and distinctiveness have been clearly defined can promotional tools be developed and reach maximum effectiveness. This is all the more so when you market to a series of countries. Mistakes can have serious effects, perhaps even destroying the prospects for a brand in a market.

In order to develop a consistent European brand strategy, have a clear vision of who will buy the brand and what character it should project, including its position and personality. Also, how the brand will be managed is an important issue. While there is no single right way of doing things, it is best developed by a small policy setting task force consisting of staff members who are intimately acquainted with the brand and all aspects relating to it.

The team members should ask themselves:

- With what do you want your customers to identify your product?
- Do you want to stress the products' benefits, the origin, the quality?

These are important questions that need to be answered and communicated in a coherent manner which is valid in all the markets you intend to penetrate.

Having set objectives the same team will need to be responsible for ensuring promotional activity is equally consistent. They should always remember it is much easier to have one agency produce a campaign which can be tailored by different offices, as opposed to using a series of independent agencies with differing corporate cultures. Remember that positioning forms the core of your communications programme. Being sensitive to what is and is not acceptable to different consumers is a golden rule. Should this involve stressing different aspects of your product according to the country, the core concept should be kept intact.

A consistent brand strategy

What is a brand?

A brand is a name, term, symbol, design, or some combination of these used to identify the products of one firm and differentiate them from the competition.

Using the same brand name and similar packaging in the whole European market, even if there are product adaptations, is increasingly becoming common practice among businesses. However, using the same brand name throughout Europe and having a European brand strategy is not the same thing.

To promote your product across Europe you need to project the same vision everywhere. This vision must be shared by everyone involved in implementing the communications programme in its various forms. Developing a European brand strategy will probably require outside consultancy from an advertising agency or specialised consultants, if only because they should know what pitfalls to avoid.

Design

EuroMarketing requires the use of visual images wherever possible, so as to cut across language and cultural barriers. Design, be it for packaging, literature or both, is a powerful tool because it can communicate across countries and cultures with unique clarity and consistency. Probably, your first experience with design was your company logo. Through this, you know design is important because it reveals a lot about your company. It makes an enduring statement about you to a wide range of audiences.

The key elements of a successful design project include:

- setting clear objectives;
- selecting the right consultancy with which to work;
- developing a meaningful brief;
- addressing contractual issues properly such as copyright, the cost of registering designs, fee structures, etc;
- managing the internal project team effectively;
- managing the design consultancy and evaluating the results.

A design project can be broken down into three stages: research, design concept and implementation. An important part of a successful design process is checking that you are answering the needs of your market, in this case the European market. It is always advisable to undertake research before launching a new corporate or packaging design. All the more so when designing for the European market.

Coming up with the actual design will require the expertise of a design company, costly though this may seem. It includes the process of origination, development and refinement resulting in one final agreed design. At each stage, the creative work must be evaluated against the agreed objectives of the brief.

Public relations

Promoting one's company and product is becoming increasingly important. Companies that have relied on their traditional good name to maintain their position in the market are now finding out that this is no longer enough. Creating awareness about one's company and products and establishing the product's reputation and image – particularly if it is an image of high quality – will take a concerted promotional effort.

As you attempt to increase your sales in the European market, promotional activity will become progressively more important. Promotion campaigns should be linked to your sales target and objective. The question most often asked by companies is, 'How much should I spend on promotion?' Rather, the question should be, 'How much am I willing to spend to create demand and meet sales targets and profit objectives?'

Having a single communications policy will allow you to integrate your promotional activities and so extend the reach of your communications. Reinforcing the message with different forms of promotion will boost the effectiveness of your effort. Public relations activity in advance of an advertising or sales promotion campaign can start building awareness and anticipation in the minds of your target audience. In this way you can attract far greater attention than either campaign would achieve alone.

Promotional literature

Whether you sell to businesses or individual customers, you will almost certainly have some literature describing your company and its products. If promotional material is not yet in the language of your target market it must be translated. Remember, the additional expense of an expert translation is preferable to the negative impression which a piece of poorly translated copy can give. Corporate literature does not need to be a work of art but obviously should be well designed and written. It should create a lasting impression of the company, setting it apart from its competitors, creating an image which a potential customer is likely to retain subconsciously.

Trade exhibitions

For selling business-to-business, there are many trade exhibitions and shows held throughout Europe which provide excellent opportunities to make your company's product or service better known and at a reasonable cost, but adequate preparation is vital. Groundwork needs to begin several months before the exhibition takes place. Otherwise, there is always the danger that the design of the stand, and the impression it gives, will not fit with the image you are trying to project. It helps if you can highlight any particular qualifications possessed, such as quality assurance certification. It is essential to make sure that all those who will be manning the stand have adequate knowledge of what is being displayed and the overall marketing objectives, as well as being properly trained in the techniques required to operate successfully at an exhibition. There are a number of good training films on this subject.

If a database of potential customers in other countries already exists, they should be sent details in advance of what the company is planning to show. Alternatively, or in addition, the exhibition organisers should be contacted to identify potential customers who are exhibiting or simply attending the event. They too should be contacted well in advance, preferably with a follow-up mail shot or, if very important, a telephone call, being made in the days immediately preceding the event.

Trade publications

The same systematic approach needs to be adopted in respect of the trade publications in the target countries. These always preview the important trade exhibitions but they need information well in advance. Press releases, which need to be translated accurately, may need to be sent two to three months before the exhibition takes place. This is worth checking. Also, do not forget the added value of relevant photographs of good quality. An invitation to representatives of the publication to attend your stand could also be included with the mailing. Finally, make sure press packs are available in either the exhibition organiser's office or the press centre, should there be one.

Videos

Correctly used, a video is a highly effective way to attract visitors, particularly at exhibitions, and to explain product benefits in a concise, visually arresting way. Producing a video need not be an expensive undertaking if

EuroMarketing

planned correctly, but it requires a co-ordinated approach. It is a good idea to ensure that the video can be used for purposes other than the exhibition such as staff training, one-to-one customer presentations or media demonstrations. Producing a video with such a multipurpose application can more than justify the investment.

Use mainly or exclusively 'voice-overs' (background commentary) and, if possible, none or very few verbal on-camera presentations. In this way you only need to produce one version for use throughout Europe, changing only the commentary to the language of your key target market. It may well pay to consider making any written texts which appear multilingual from the start.

Speaking opportunities

Many exhibitions provide seminars or workshops where visitors can hear about new developments or debate important industry issues. This provides another opportunity for company promotion. You should consider offering your company's assistance either as a co-sponsor of the seminar, or more simply, by offering one of your staff as a speaker. This will help position your company as a spokesperson for the industry, raising your credibility among potential customers. There may be an additional benefit in that such seminars are often reported in the trade press, but remember to have a copy of the presentation available if you want an accurate record to appear. Do make sure that the person designated by you knows the subject, is a compelling speaker and has something positive to impart. Otherwise the whole exercise can have the makings of a public relations disaster.

Sponsorship

A company should also look at other sponsorship opportunities. Many exhibitions, for example, will have a newsletter published every day and it may be possible to sponsor the publication itself, or a section of it. The same principle applies to the official catalogue, or to promotional mailings by the organisers in advance of the exhibition. These sponsorships tend to be inexpensive and they provide easily accessible ways to raise your company's profile. Sporting and cultural events also exist which give similar opportunities for relatively inexpensive sponsorship. Your public relations consultants should be able to provide details.

Sales promotion

As sales promotion, unlike media advertising, acts at the point-of-sale it is normally used as a short-term tactical weapon. That is to achieve specific marketing objectives during a defined time period. While consisting of a series of relatively short-term initiatives it is usually an integral part of a brand's long-term strategy.

Sales promotion can have a very strategic role to play in helping to build a brand and to reflect a strong advertising message. Where the volume of media advertising is going to be limited its use will be even more essential. For consumer products it clarifies perceptions of the benefits provided at the crucial point of decision as to whether or not to buy. One promotional concept and visual image can easily be adapted for other markets. The retailers in the target countries may use these materials in different ways but it is possible to accommodate their needs within a common concept so the essential message remains unchanged. Materials can also be produced and given to the retailer or business partner and co-branded by him by overprinting logos etc. to reinforce the partnership in the mind of the consumer and to help stimulate greater acceptance. For sales promotion to be effective on a pan-European basis it is essential to devise a strong promotional offer and to ensure that the correct brand message is maintained in each market, with an accurate and idiomatic translation of copy.

Some of the really big brands are now running pan-European promotions, albeit with variations for each local market. Most businesses have yet to organise themselves to do likewise. One reason may be the initial cost of so doing. What must be kept in mind is that you, unlike the large multinationals, will only be trying to enter one market at a time. The objective must be to ensure that you do not have to redesign all your promotional materials each time you try to extend your activities to another country. So, planning ahead, while possibly costly in the short-term, should save money in the end.

It should be remembered that fully integrated pan-European activity is very difficult to achieve, partly due to different national legislation, which must be adhered to. Knowledge of both national legislation, sales promotional practices and cultural factors is frequently only possessed by the marketing departments of large companies or sales promotion practitioners and consultants who are familiar with the market, or with similar products in the market. At present, there are very few organisations equipped to help you run promotions across Europe. By linking into an international promotional network having local operators familiar with market nuances, you stand a better chance of being provided with a campaign showing an acceptable level of quality.

Advertising

Prior reference has already been made to the subject of advertising, but it has still to be pointed out that pan-European advertising opportunities are emerging. Every day one can now see advertisements which are being used in a number of countries without alteration, or with simple language adaptations.

Using advertising should be considered seriously when entering new territories in order to support the sales effort, even if this has not been the normal practice in your home market. This is because you need to build credibility, something you hopefully already enjoy at home.

Direct mail

Direct mail can be a very cost-efficient means of reaching a limited number of potential customers, who may be geographically dispersed. It can also be used to keep in direct contact with existing customers, particularly when used as a medium for distributing a company newsletter. It is, however, a specialised field of activity with many lessons needing to be learned before it can be used effectively. You would be well advised to seek specialised advice on this subject unless you are already experienced in its use. The use of such specialist assistance can double or treble the effectiveness of a direct mail campaign.

Promotional Policy

To do

First ensure your communications programme is consistent with your positioning statement and decide how it can be used with the minimum of adaptation in all the markets you will eventually be targeting.

_____

_____

_____

_____

_____

Ask yourself

- Do you have the same brand strategy for each market?
- For each country, does the brand have the same positioning, personality, role, history? If it is not the same everywhere, can clusters of similarity be identified?
- How is the brand management to be organised?
- Who is going to lead the company's move towards European brand management if such a strategy is not already in place?
- What external assistance is going to be required in order to carry out your policies?

On the next pages set out the main headings of all the actions required in order to develop your branding strategy for Europe, detailing where you will need external assistance. It would be advisable to supplement this with a timetable setting out the dates by which each stage of the process is to be achieved.

EuroMarketing

Your branding strategy for Europe

Promotional Policy

The timetable for completing your branding strategy

CHAPTER 11

DEVELOPING, IMPLEMENTING AND EVALUATING YOUR EUROMARKETING STRATEGY

Rolling out

Coast-to-coast ...

If you want to learn about marketing in a single market, ask the managers of companies in a country where this situation has existed for over a hundred years. That is, ever since the development of communications provided access to the varying regional markets in the US, wherever the company was located. US SMEs do not ask if they should standardise their marketing or not, they do it automatically. Their concern is with choosing the best method by which to standardise.

Although most US firms only operate in one or two marketing regions, coast-to-coast marketing is the objective of ambitious SMEs in the US. The most dynamic and successful use a roll-out strategy – a strategy which is increasingly being used in Europe.

'Roll-out marketing' refers to a process which involves experimenting with the best way to market a product, using a test market to gain experience, and following its refinement, 'rolling-out' the marketing campaign across the continent. Expansion is achieved by focusing on one region at a time and heavily promoting the product or service. Profits earned in one region are invested in the marketing effort in the next. This process is

Developing, Implementing and Evaluating

repeated until the marketing campaign extends throughout the nation.

The examples given below illustrate the effectiveness of such an integrated, standardised strategy.

Vermont Teddy Bear: experimenting

A good example of the use of a roll-out strategy is by a firm called Vermont Teddy Bear, which was selling its teddy bears through toy shops in New England. They discovered that there was no way to get shelf space specifically allocated to their bears, who were dressed in costumes for special occasions. Furthermore the retail mark-up left no profit to do any direct consumer advertising. So, Vermont Teddy Bear experimented with advertising on one radio station in Boston to encourage direct purchases of 'special occasion' teddy bears. The medium of radio allowed the company to tell its story in a lively manner. It now had available for investment in advertising the margin previously allowed to retailers and, by using it, was able to generate an instant response.

The first test was so successful that Vermont Teddy Bear decided to use several radio stations in Boston. It has now expanded across the country, one major city at a time, using the profits from each prior city to finance both the expanded radio advertising and the expansion of production, transport and the increased number of telephone operators needed to take orders. It is also expanding its product line so that it has bears for any occasion and can sell all year round.

Despite this US success story, care is required when employing the same strategy in Europe, unless you are prepared to abandon your existing retailer base. On this side of the water many retailers consider direct selling to consumers by their suppliers as disloyal and constituting an unfair business practice.

Pace

Pace, Inc. is an SME which makes a line of products including Pace Salsa (a hot Mexican-type pepper sauce now extremely popular in the US and selling in high volumes) sold originally in San Antonio, Texas. They began by expanding to Dallas, then Houston, then Oklahoma, then New Mexico.

The roll-out strategy depended on focusing substantially more resources in each new market than allocated by the competition. In each new market they spent three times as much on advertising during the introduction than all their competitors combined – including the well-established food giants!

EuroMarketing

They set up sampling points in stores and gave small sample jars to butchers to be given to their best customers. They then appointed an established local food broker (distributor) to serve the market. The location of their next roll-out city was chosen by the amount of mail received from people who had purchased the Pace Salsa while on a visit to one of their current marketing areas and had written to ask where they could buy it in their own locality. They now have national distribution and are the largest Salsa producer in the US.

Only recently the company was sold to a major food company for over US$1 billion. This indicates the large rewards available to even small firms who can successfully operate a roll-out strategy. Over 400 fast growing smaller companies secure an initial listing for their shares on the US NASDAQ electronic stock market each year, and only about 20 per cent of these can be classified as falling into the high technology sector. The others have achieved their success by meeting market needs in a consistent and structured fashion. It can be anticipated that the number of similar European success stories will increase progressively as more and more businesses take advantage of the European Single Market.

Summer Roll Out: outspending the competition on promotion

Another success story comes from a manufacturer who invented a new liquid lawn fertiliser. It was the company's first branded product sold under their own name and was initially test marketed in the state where the company was based using TV advertising and selling direct to the retailers. This did not bring the required results, and the company decided it could sell on a national basis without using traditional hardware distributors. Instead, by selling direct to retailers it would have enough margin to more than double the amount of advertising in each market, which was quite important given this was a seasonal product, not one bought throughout the year.

A three-year roll-out plan was designed. Each year the company would enter a new territory and saturate that area with TV advertising during the peak lawn fertiliser purchasing period in the spring. This heavy advertising not only generated sales but also got the company into nearly every major sales outlet. The profits from each prior year were used to expand in the next year. The advertising in the second year in each market could be reduced from the amount spent in the launch year, while achieving a similar impact. Once the company was national, its total TV advertising cost was no more than it had spent in launching its product in a new region.

Engineering Success: Experimenting

A supplier of engineering services to *Fortune 1000* companies (the top 1000 gross earning companies in the US) began selling the equipment required in order to provide its service. It used its direct salesforce and a catalogue listing the items and prices. The company was competing against established office supply retailers that also carried certain pieces of engineering equipment, but it had an advantage: many of the items were thinly distributed, because office supply retailers only carried fast moving lines, which were hard to find in their large catalogues.

The response was so encouraging that the company investigated ways to market the line to enterprises not already targeted by its salesforce. The list of potential buyers was extremely long and the salesforce could not call on all of them. So an experiment was tried using mailing lists, sending out an improved direct response catalogue. The response rate for some of the lists was good so they formed a new division to sell a full line of products and associated training seminars through direct mail.

They continued to experiment with different lists until they found the ones with high response rates and used only those. They also looked at how often they should mail and eventually decided on a frequency of twice a year to the full list and four times a year to any customer that had purchased an item in the previous year. As the catalogue became known, the product line grew. Also, manufacturers began approaching them, asking that their products be included in the catalogue.

Franchising carpet cleaners

An entire industry has grown up to assist companies that want to franchise what they have developed. There are consulting firms to help write the system documents, specialist law firms to register the franchise in each US state (each state has different laws regulating franchising) and marketing consultants who help to market the franchise.

One example is a company that developed a new way to sell carpet cleaning. It developed a franchising package and sold it by advertising in small business magazines and participating in small business opportunity shows, which are held in most major cities around the country. It then developed a new way to sell carpets from a truck which went directly to the consumer's home. Initially they sold this new franchise in the same way as their existing one. When sufficient franchises were established, they began to advertise on nationally syndicated radio. Radio allowed them to tell their full story and to describe their advantages over existing retail outlets. This not only increased sales of carpets, but the number of franchise inquiries.

Now consider ...

What lessons can be learned from the US experience of operating this exciting technique of 'roll out' marketing? Note that while the methods used were different, each involved the development of an approach with distinctive features. In every case the marketing approach was a fully integrated one, developed on the basis of extensive market research and testing.

Remember that both trade buyers and end-consumers tend to be relatively more resistant to selling messages than do their counterparts in the US. This requires you to be both credible and highly persuasive. Original concepts, including new methods of distribution, can be highly successful in Europe and some translate from the US, as firms such as Dell Computers have shown. There are, however, plenty of examples where they have not, and the total 'roll-out' marketing package needs thoroughly preparing, and testing in a limited area, before being employed as a standard technique to extend the range of markets you serve.

Organising for Europe

Pagh Morup

'Exporting in Europe is easier than most people think – just have a go at it', says the managing director of Pagh Morup, a Danish clothing contractor. It was not always an easy task for him though. In the early 1970s, the owner finally decided that having 150 different clients was becoming too burdensome. It was decided to standardise their marketing strategy and streamline the client list, serving only those which they considered had long-term potential. Today, they have achieved an annual turnover of 38 m ECU, of which exports account for 95 per cent, with a total administrative staff of only 23 people including assistants. A centralised structure for the firm was chosen to be able to make decisions without bureaucratic delay. Real power lies in the hands of only a few people and this centralisation makes it easier to plan and implement a standardised strategy.

Developing, Implementing and Evaluating

As this example shows, taking full advantage of the Single Market may require the reorganisation of your current marketing objectives and sales activities. As your marketing becomes more planned, and positive results in the terms of additional revenue begin to emerge, the creation of a specialist marketing department may have to be considered. At the very least the centralisation and control of your marketing operation will be essential for a successful implementation of your EuroMarketing strategy.

Most SMEs implementing a EuroMarketing strategy have delegated the marketing responsibility to a special task force or a manager. Experience shows the greater the centralisation of decision making concerned with setting policies and allocating resources, the more effective is the implementation of a standardised EuroMarketing approach.

In addition, marketing, just as with finance and production, must be regarded as being worthy of the attention of top management, and as an essential tool in achieving the strategic objectives of the company. It must be taken out of a corner of the sales office and brought into the boardroom. Otherwise it will be impossible to develop a successful EuroMarketing strategy.

CHAPTER 12

IN CONCLUSION

EuroMarketing

As you will by now be all too aware, marketing in your regional or national market and marketing in the Single Market of 370 million consumers are very different. Whereas in your national market you may well have only conducted very limited research, relying largely on personal instinct and experience, the larger market requires systematic research into your own position, the needs of your customers and the activities of your competitors. To rely on instinct when you have only limited experience of another country would be unwise, to say the least.

Whereas in your national market you may have been able to get away with 'common sense' marketing, maybe even without having a full-time marketing manager or a marketing plan, strategic planning is a key prerequisite for success in EuroMarketing. In short, unless you are simply fortunate, there is not much chance of success without:

- good research;
- strategic planning;
- strict implementation of the marketing strategy once devised and tested;
- constant monitoring and evaluation of the marketing process and its results;
- regular correction of the marketing strategy in the light of the evaluation.

In Conclusion

To prepare a EuroMarketing plan and to carry it out is a major undertaking. On the other hand the opportunities and threats created by the Single Market are very significant. How large they will be no one can yet predict but many businesses will feel the effect. Those that plan properly are those that are most likely to be in a position to celebrate the arrival of the year 2000. Others who try to ignore current market developments may well not be so fortunate.

Having worked through the book to this point clearly places you in the former category, showing you to be a progressive and entrepreneurial manager willing to invest in the future. Hopefully the pointers given, coupled with the hard work you have done, will place you in a good position to reap your just reward.

This will only come about, however, if you appreciate that the development of a coherent marketing strategy, whether or not it can be termed EuroMarketing in its purest sense, is not the end of the matter. Legislation affecting your activities will continue to be tabled, judgements issued by the Court of Justice which may change the way existing legislation is interpreted, new technological advances will be made, new services offered.

Your marketing will only continue to be relevant if your business keeps up with events as they evolve. Someone within your organisation will have to have this task delegated to them, with the responsibility to report developments regularly, together with their likely effects on the organisation, to the chief executive and any others directly involved.

Despite the constant change with which all businesses seemingly have to cope nowadays, it is certain that the individual Member States, and regions within them, will continue to display cultural diversity and differences in taste. In such circumstances, Europe will have the fortunate combination of a growing economy coupled with a rich quality of life. This offers magnificent opportunities to those prepared to develop a marketing approach that standardises where there are similarities, but takes account of the realities where differences exist.

APPENDIX A

THE SINGLE MARKET, AN UPDATE BY SECTOR

Note: only those sectors thought to be of interest to the majority of businesses likely to be developing a EuroMarketing programme have been included. This appendix should not be treated as if it constituted a complete or comprehensive review of the situation.

Value added tax

Most companies trading across frontiers report that the current system for value added tax (VAT) has brought them considerable savings in terms of reduction of transport costs, abolition of the pre-payment of VAT on intra-Community imports, and the elimination of charges concerned with customs formalities. Smaller firms have, however, found that the systems imposed extra accounting costs upon them at the introductory stage. Remaining problems concern the coexistence of divergent national systems, the difficulties of carrying out transactions in a Member State where the trader is not established, the special conditions that apply to distance selling (typically mail order), and with certain categories of transactions (for example chain transactions).

While the European Commission is now discussing with all those concerned the options for creating a unified and final system of value added tax this is taking longer than anticipated. For the present, plans should be based on coping with the present system.

Company taxation

Little or no progress has been made because of a lack of agreement between the Member States. Any operations carried out in another Member State will be subject to the rules of the double taxation agreement between that country and the one in which your business is legally established. Where matters such as payments of interest and fees for the use of intellectual property rights are concerned, it is always essential to take proper legal advice before entering into any form of agreement.

Mutual recognition of professional qualifications

The small number of complaints received by the European Commission would indicate that the current system is working relatively well. There is, however, the intention to take measures to further enhance mutual recognition of a wider spectrum of qualifications possessed by skilled tradespeople.

The free movement of persons/right of establishment

Unless contemplating establishing a subsidiary, creating a branch, or directly employing someone in another country, this will not be a matter requiring consideration. Should any of these actions be under discussion, it should be noted that difficult problems can arise in certain instances. Seeking professional advice, legal and fiscal, before any action is taken is essential.

Technical barriers to trade

This term is a form of administrative shorthand used to describe those national regulations which, through imposing additional testing, certification or other requirements, can make it more difficult and expensive to enter a market. The failure at the national level to properly apply 'mutual recognition', that is allowing goods legally put on the market in another Member State to freely circulate in another, frequently gives rise to problems of market access which should no longer arise. Apart from those areas where harmonised legislation exists, the intention has always been that other products should generally be allowed to circulate freely, and be placed on other markets without additional testing, always providing they have been adequately tested in their country of origin. Too often, national authorities are still requiring the carrying out of additional formalities, which can be costly and time consuming. Particular problems have been noted in relation to road vehicles, foodstuffs and pharmaceuticals, although it is known that many other types of product can be required, on the basis of safeguarding the health of workers or the public, to undergo additional certification procedures. When examining the possibility of entering a market it is important to find out whether any national certification, testing or other requirements apply to your products or services.

There is currently a proposal before the Council of Ministers and the European Parliament to require a Member State to inform both the European Commission and other Member States of any decisions taken to refuse the free movement of goods legally manufactured and/or marketed in another Member State. If this measure is finally agreed to, it should progressively reduce the number of national barriers to market entry which currently exist.

European technical product standardisation

Community legislation in this field is based on what are called framework directives. These set out those requirements which are regarded as essential if the product is to conform with its provisions. Should they do so the products concerned will be required to bear the CE Marking, and will then be able to circulate freely throughout the European Union. Examples of such directives include those relating to machine safety, personal protective equipment and gas appliances.

This framework legislation is supported by a series of product standards drawn up by the European standardisation bodies. These are located in Brussels but are independent of the European Commission, which is effectively one of their customers. When they are asked to draw up a new standard, on the basis of what is called a mandate, they establish one or more technical committees, composed of experts from industry, in order to carry out the work. Once a draft standard has been prepared and subjected to a public enquiry, it is then voted upon by the national standards bodies. If they approve, which can be on the basis of majority voting, it becomes a European standard. These do not have any force until they are transposed into national standards by the national bodies.

If you have products subject to one of these standards, you should already be aware of the consequent withdrawal of the previous national standard by your national standardisation body and the issuing of a new one replicating the European standard, and will no doubt have adapted your products accordingly. Problems arise where a standard is in course of preparation, but not finalised, or is planned, but work on drawing it up has not yet begun. There are several thousand falling into one or other of these categories.

Eventually there could be ten thousand or more European standards, although four-fifths of these will be drawn up as a result of initiatives by those involved in a sector of activity rather than being strictly part of the Single Market programme. Nevertheless, it is important for you to know if any new European standards are likely to affect your products, and within what timescale, or whether you will have to contend with a series of varying national standards, with associated certification requirements, into the indefinite future. This is a factor which, if relevant, can have a significant bearing on which new geographical markets to attack. Information on standardisation matters can normally be obtained from your trade association, or failing that, the national standardisation body.

Intellectual property

When seeking to enter new markets a question of primary importance is how to ensure that all intellectual property rights possessed by your company, that is trademarks, patents, design rights and copyrightable materials, enjoy the fullest practicable degree of legal protection. This is probably best achieved through making use of the integrated facilities now becoming progressively available within the European Union.

The protection of intellectual property is a complex subject requiring advice from a specialist in the appropriate field but the following outline of the structures that now exist, or are likely to in the future, may be of assistance.

Action by the Commission in this field focused initially on trade marks. The measures adopted had two objectives. First, to create a Community trade mark. Second, to harmonise the laws applying to national trade marks. The basic regulation on a Community trade mark was approved by the Council of Ministers on 20 December 1993. This will allow firms to market their products throughout the EU on the basis of protection achieved through a single registration. A European trade mark office has been established in Alicante, Spain. A further proposal for a directive seeks

EuroMarketing

to change the way national marks are registered, and the rights conferred by such registration bring these in line with the arrangements set out in the basic regulation mentioned above.

A similar approach has been taken in respect of design rights. Two proposals are currently under discussion, one aimed at introducing the concept of an EU design, the other approximating existing national laws.

When it comes to patents two international conventions exist. The first, the Munich Convention on the European Patent, which was signed in 1973 by a number of Member States and European non-member countries, provides for patents to be granted in a number of countries on the basis of one application to a European Patent Office, which is independent of the European Commission. All Member States are now parties to this convention. The Luxembourg Convention, which was signed in 1989, aimed to provide equivalent effect for European Patents in all the Member States. This is not yet in force as some of the signatories have yet to ratify it.

In the field of copyright and related rights, and in order to adapt existing intellectual property systems to the technological changes now taking place in fields such as software, micro-circuits and biotechnology, five directives have been adopted. These seek to protect:

- the intellectual property content of computer chip designs;
- the contents of computer programmes;
- rental and lending rights in the field of intellectual property;
- material broadcast from satellites and re-transmitted by cable; and
- copyright and related rights by harmonising the period of protection.

A number of other proposals for directives are currently being examined and should be approved over the coming months. Given the decision of the European Parliament to reject the amended draft directive concerning the legal protection of biological inventions, these will remain subject to national rules for the foreseeable future.

Public procurement

All contracts above a certain size are now subject to harmonised rules, although some have yet to be incorporated into national legislation. When all are in place this will increase the opportunities for winning contracts

The Single Market: An Update by Sector

in other countries, but only if the most careful preparation is undertaken. This being such a specialised subject, this book does not attempt to deal with marketing products or services to public purchasers.

Remaining gaps in Community law

It might be thought that 280 separate legislative measures would have been sufficient to create a harmonised legal framework in all areas of activity likely to affect the operations of the Single Market. This is not the case, as some have still to be approved by the Council of Ministers. There are also still significant gaps, of which it is important to be aware:

- the failure to adopt measures proposed to remove border controls on people;
- the absence of fiscal harmonisation in some fields, particularly the tax treatment of businesses operating in more than one Member State;
- delays in adapting company law to single market requirements, coupled with the continued failure to agree a convention on insolvency;
- insufficient liberalisation in certain sectors, notably telecommunications and energy, although significant progress is now being made with regard to telecommunications;
- absence of a single European currency, with the resulting exchange risks affecting cross-border transactions.

Future developments

The European Commission has already announced its intention to take certain further measures in the near future. These are in addition to improving administrative co-operation between the Member States and achieving better observance of the concept of mutual recognition. They include:

- providing citizens with better rights of redress as consumers;
- preparing for a cross-border information society;
- supporting the creation of trans-European networks in the fields of transport and information technology;

EuroMarketing

- better integration of Single Market, social and environmental objectives;
- assisting Central and Eastern Europe to adapt to Single Market requirements;
- ensure equivalent enforcement, including types of penalty, for infringements of Single Market legislation.
- acting on cross-border money transfer costs and delays in payment.

A number of these proposed initiatives could have implications for the marketing strategy you intend to develop. For example, would the proposed new transport networks affect the way you undertook your distribution? Will your means of electronic communication be adequate? Should Central and Eastern Europe be regarded as being an opportunity or a threat?

Again, only you can answer questions of this type – but they should be asked.

APPENDIX B

EURO INFO CENTRES: A CONTACT LIST

Austria

Euro Info Centre
Wirtschaftskammer Österreich
Wiedner Hauptstrasse, 63
Postfach 152
1045   Vienna
Austria

Contact   Mr Walter RESL
Tel   43 1 501054191
Fax   43 1 50206297
Web site   www.wk.or.at/ih_info/eu-home.htm
E-mail   eic@wk.or.at

Euro Info Centre
Industriellenvereinigung
Schwarzenbergplatz 4
Postfach 61
1031   Vienna
Austria

Contact   Mr Christian MANDL
Tel   43 1 711352405
Fax   43 1 711352914
Web site   www.telecom.at/eic
E-mail   christian.mandl@voei.ada.at

Euro Info Centre
Wiener Wirtschaftsförderungsfonds
Ebendorferstraße 2
1082   Vienna
Austria

Contact   Ms Monika UNTERHOLZNER
Tel   43 1 400086173
Fax   43 1 40007071

EuroMarketing

Euro Info Centre
Wirtschaftskammer Salzburg
Julius-Raab-Platz 1
5027   Salzburg
Austria

Contact   Ms Martina SCHERTHANNER
Tel   43 662 451327
Fax   43 662 454889
E-mail   hafe@tzs.co.at

Euro Info Centre
Wirtschaftskammer Oberösterreich
Mozartstaße 20
4020   Linz
Austria

Contact   Mr Robert LEITNER
Tel   43 732 7800479
Fax   43 732 7800642
E-mail   eicooe@wkooe.wk.or.at

Euro Info Centre
Wirtschaftskammer Steiermark
Körblergasse 111-113
Postfach 1038
8021   Graz
Austria

Contact   Ms Claudia WEYRINGER
Tel   43 316 601600
Fax   43 316 601535
E-mail   weyring@wk.stmk.wk.or.at

Euro Info Centre
Wirtschaftskammer Tirol
Meinhardstraße 14
6020   Innsbruck
Austria

Contact   Mr Peter VÖLKER
Tel   43 512 5310221
Fax   43 512 5310275
E-mail   pvoelker@aw.tirol.wk.or.at

Euro Info Centres

Belgium

Euro Info Centre
Bureau Economique de la Province
de Namur (B.E.P.N.)
Avenue Sergent Vrithoff, 2
5000   Namur
Belgium

Contact   M. Bernard RUYSSEN
Tel   32 81 735209
Fax   32 81 742945
Telex   59101
E-mail   bepnri@pophost.eunet.be

Euro Info Centre
Kamer van Koophandel en
Nijverheid van Antwerpen
Markgravestraat, 12
2000   Antwerp
Belgium

Contact   Mr Luc LUWEL
Tel   32 3 2322219
Fax   32 3 2336442

Euro Info Centre
C.D.P. – Idelux
Drève de l'Arc-en-Ciel, 98
6700   Arlon
Belgium

Contact   M. Pierre MARTIN
Tel   32 63 231875
Fax   32 63 231895

Euro Info Centre
Chambre de Commerce et
d'Industrie de Bruxelles/Fabrimétal
Avenue Louise, 500
1050   Brussels
Belgium

Contact   M Luc DE WOLF
Tel   32 2 6485873
Fax   32 2 6409328
Web site   www.cci.be/brussels
E-mail   ccibrussels@cci.be

Euro Info Centre
Ministerie van de Vlaamse
Gemeenschap
Administratie Economie
Markiesstraat, 1
1000   Brussels
Belgium

Contact   Mme. Iris DENOLF
Tel   32 2 5073730
Fax   32 2 5024702

EuroMarketing

Euro Info Centre	Contact	M. Philippe CHEVREMONT
Euroguichet Hainaut-Est		
Avenue Général Michel, 1E	Tel	32 71 331460
6000 Charleroi	Fax	32 71 316735
Belgium	E-mail	heracles@heracles.charline.be

Euro Info Centre	Contact	M. Johan DECLERCK
van de Vlaamse Gom's	Tel	32 9 2215511
Floralia Paleis Congrescentrum,	Fax	32 9 2215500
bus 6	Telex	12 666
9000 Gent	E-mail	be1007_gent@vans.infonet.com
Belgium		

Euro Info Centre	Contact	Mme. Ingrid FLEURQUIN
Kamer voor Handel en Nijverheid		
van Limburg	Tel	32 11 284400
Gouverneur Roppesingel, 51	Fax	32 11 284406
3500 Hasselt		
Belgium		

Euro Info Centre	Contact	M. Walter BORMS
NCMV Internationaal	Tel	32 56 224123
Lange Steenstraat, 10	Fax	32 56 229694
8500 Kortrijk		
Belgium		

Euro Info Centre	Contact	Mme. Monique ROVER
Institut Provincial des Classes		
Moyennes	Tel	32 41 201111
Le Vertbois	Fax	32 41 201120
Rue du Vertbois, 13 A	Telex	42 037 IPCM-B
4000 Liège	E-mail	ipcm@mail.interpac.be
Belgium		

Euro Info Centres

Euro Info Centre Hainaut Site du Grand Hornu Rue Sainte Louise, 82 7301 Hornu (Mons) Belgium	Contact M. Thierry MATON Tel 32 65 777970 Fax 32 65 779091
Euro Info Centre Brussels Airport Kamer voor Handel en Nijverheid Halle-Vilvoorde Brucargo Gebouw, 706 Lokaal 7614 1931 Zaventem Belgium	Contact M. Wim VAN GENECHTEN Tel 32 2 7519056 Fax 32 2 7517811 Web site www.cci.be/hv E-mail ccihv@cci.be
Euro Info Centre (Antenne de BE-010 Liège) Stellenvermittlungsamt Arbeitsbeschassung – Forem Borngasse, 3–5 4700 Eupen Belgium	Contact Mlle. Brigitte FIJALKOWSKI Tel 32 87 742180 Fax 32 87 557085
Euro Info Centre (Antenne de BEIOII-Mons) Chambre de Commerce et d'Industrie du Tournaisis Rue Beyaert, 75 7500 Tournai Belgium	Contact Mme. Isabelle WALSCHAP Tel 32 69 221121 Fax 32 69 212784
Euro Info Centre ARIES Association 'Réseau d'Information de l'Economie Sociale' 51, rue de la Concorde 1050 Brussels Belgium	Contact M. Gilles DEMBLON Tel 32 2 5137501 Fax 32 2 5123265 Web site www.poptel.org.uk/aries E-mail aries-g.demblon@geo2. poptel.org.uk

EuroMarketing

Denmark

Euro Info Centre
Århus
Amts Kommune
Haslegaardsvænget 18-20
8210   Århus
Denmark

Contact   Mr Henrick Michael
            JENSEN
Tel   45 86152577
Fax   45 86154322
E-mail   lieu051@inet.uni-c.dk

Euro Info Centre Fyn
Fyns Erhvervsråd
Blangstedgaardsvej, 1
5220   Odense SOE
Denmark

Contact   Mr Ole FUGLSANG
Tel   45 66156531
Fax   45 66156541

Euro Info Centre
Sønderjyllands Erhversråd
Bjerggade 4 L
6200   Aabenraa
Denmark

Contact   Mr Leif SCHØLER
Tel   45 74622384
Fax   45 74626760
E-mail   sdj.erhvraad@po.ia.dk

Euro Info Centre
Herning
Birk Centerpark 7
7400   Herning
Denmark

Contact   Ms Hanne Thaarup
            MØLBAK
Tel   45 97129200
Fax   45 97129244

Euro Info Centre
Danish Technological Institute (DTI)
Gregersensvej
Postbox 141
2630   Copenhagen-Tåstrup
Denmark

Contact   Ms Nils THYSSEN
Tel   45 43504000
Fax   45 43716360
Web site euroweb.dti.dk
E-mail   euro@dti.dk

Euro Info Centres

Euro Info Centre
Det Danske Handelskammer
Børsen
1217   Copenhagen
Denmark

Contact Mr Bo GREEN
Tel   45 33950500
Fax   45 33325216

Euro Info Centre
Håndværksrådet – Viborg A/S
Lille Sankt Hansgade 20
8800   Viborg
Denmark

Contact Ms Annette
            NEDEGAARD
Tel   45 86627711
Fax   45 86614921

Euro Info Centre Størstroms
Marienbergvej 80
4760   Vordingborg
Denmark

Contact Ms Grethe
            LAMBRECHT
Tel   45 55340155
Fax   45 55340355
E-mail   seic@post3.tele.dk

EuroMarketing

Finland

Euro Info Centre
The Finnish Foreign Trade
Association
Arkadiankatu, 2
P.O. Box 908
00101   Helsinki
Finland

Contact Mr Taisto SULONEN
Tel   358 0 1992
Fax   358 204 695535
Web site www.exports.finland.fi
E-mail   info@exports.finland.fi

Euro Info Centre North Finland
Ministry of Trade and Industry
Regional Business Service Office
in Oulu
Asemakatu, 37
90100
Finland

Contact Ms Riitta HEIKKINEN
Tel   358 81 3160220
Fax   358 81 3160221
E-mail   riitta.heikkinen@oyt.
         oulu.fi

Euro Info Centre
Lahti Chamber of Commerce
South Karelia Chamber of Commerce
Neopoli Niemenkatu, 73
15210   Lahti
Finland

Contact Ms Marjatta PASILA
Tel   358 18 8114208
Fax   358 18 7511524

Euro Info Centre Botnia
Ostrobothnia Chamber of Commerce
Raastuvankatu, 20
65100   Vaasa
Finland

Contact Mr Juha HÄKKINEN
Tel   358 61 3172279
Fax   358 61 3126656
Web site www.multi.fi/eicbotnia
E-mail   eicbotnia@multi.fi

Euro Info Centre
Kuopio Chamber of Commerce
Kasarmikatu, 2
70110   Kuopio
Finland

Contact Mr Matti NIIRANEN
Tel   358 71 2820291
Fax   358 71 2823304

Euro Info Centres

Euro Info Centre Turku
MTI Regional Business Service
Office in Turku (South West Finland)
20100   Turku
Finland

Contact   Mr Jyri ARPONEN
Tel   358 21 2510051
Fax   358 21 2310667
E-mail   satu.artiola@turku.
          yrityspalvelu.mailnet

Euro Info Centre TEKES
Technology Development Centre
Malminkatu, 34
PO Box 69
00101   Helsinki
Finland

Contact   Mr Lauri GRÖHN
Tel   358 0 69367201
Fax   358 0 69367794
Web site   www.tekes.fi
E-mail   lauri.grohn@tekes.fi/

EuroMarketing

France

Euro Info Centre Lyon-Rhône-Alpes
Chambre de Commerce et
d'Industrie de Lyon
16, Rue de la République
69289   Lyon cedex 02
France

Contact   Mme. Catherine
           JAMON-SERVEL
Tel   33 72405746
Fax   33 78379400
E-mail   fr251_lyon@vans.
           infonet.com

Euro Info Centre
Comité d'Expansion Aquitaine
2, Place de la Bourse
33076   Bordeaux cedex
France

Contact   Mme. Martine
           DRONVAL
Tel   33 56015010/09
Fax   33 56015005

Euro Info Centre
Région de Lorraine
World Trade Centre – Tour B
2, Rue Augustin Fresnel
57070   Metz
France

Contact   Mme. Patricia
           CUISINIER
Tel   33 87204090
Fax   33 87740315

Euro Info Centre Pays de la Loire
Chambres de Commerce et
d'Industrie de Nantes et de
Saint Nazaire
Centre des Salorges-BP 718
16, quai Renaud
44027   Nantes cedex 04
France

Contact   Mme. Isabelle
           CHARLOT-
           BLANCHARD
Tel   33 40446055
Fax   33 40446380
E-mail   wtcna@wtca.geis.com

Euro Info Centre
Maison du Commerce International
de Strasbourg (MCIS)
4, quai Kléber
67080   Strasbourg cedex
France

Contact   Mme. Veronique
           OBERLE
Tel   33 88764224
Fax   33 88764200

Euro Info Centres

Euro Info Centre
Chambre Régionale de Commerce
et d'Industrie de Picardie
36, rue des Otages
80037   Amiens cedex 01
France

Contact   Mme. Marie Francoise DUEE
Tel   33 22828093
Fax   33 22912904
E-mail   101534.2573@compuserve.com

Euro Info Centre
Chambre Régionale de Commerce
et d'Industrie de Franche-Comté
Valparc
Zac de Valentin
25043   Besançon
France

Contact   M. Stéphane BRUGAL
Tel   33 81804111
Fax   33 81807094

Euro Info Centre Toulouse-Blagnac
Chambre Régionale de Commerce
et d'Industrie Midi-Pyrénées
5, rue Dieudonné Costes -BP 32
31701 Toulouse-Blagnac
France

Contact   M. Jacques ALBAS
Tel   33 62742000
Fax   33 62742020
E-mail   falcou-eic@crcimp.capmedia.fr

Euro Info Centre de
Basse-Normandie
C.R.C.I. Basse-Normandie
21, place de la République
14052   Caen cedex
France

Contact   Mme. Isabelle HERAULT
Tel   33 31383167
Fax   33 31857641

Euro Info Centre
Chambre de Commerce et
d'Industrie de Guyane
Française
Place de l'Esplanade – BP 49
97321   Cayenne cedex
France

Contact   Mme. Marie Joseph PINVILLE
Tel   594 299601/299600
Fax   594 299634/299645

EuroMarketing

Euro Info Centre
Champagne-Ardenne
10, rue de Chastillon – BP 537
51010   Châlons en Champagne
France

Contact   Mme. Béatrice
             DECROUX
Tel   33 26693365
Fax   33 26704919

Euro Info Centre Auvergne
Chambre de Commerce et
d'Industrie de
Clermont-Ferrand/Issoire
148, boulevard Lavoisier
63037   Clermont-Ferrand
France

Contact   M. Bruno MASSE
Tel   33 73434332
Fax   33 73434325
E-mail   100640.562@
             compuserve.com

Euro Info Centre
Chambre Régionale de Commerce
et d'Industrie de Bourgogne
68, rue Chevreul – BP 209
21006   Dijon
France

Contact   M. Robert GUYON
Tel   33 80635263
Fax   33 80635253

Euro Info Centre
Chambre de Commerce et
d'Industrie de la Martinique
50, rue Ernest Deproge
97200   Fort de France
France

Contact   Mme. Cémiane
             MOUTOUCOUMARO
Tel   596 552825
Fax   596 716680

Euro Info Centre Nord-Pas de Calais
Centre de Documentation
185, boulevard de la Liberté
BP 2027
59013   Lille cedex
France

Contact   Mme. Dominique
             CHAUSSEC DE
             LECOUR
Tel   33 20400277
Fax   33 20400433

Euro Info Centres

Euro Info Centre
Chambre Régionale de Commerce et d'Industrie Limousin/Poitou-Charentes
Boulevard des Arcades
87038 Limoges
France

Contact M. Martin FORST
Tel 33 55044025
Fax 33 55044040

Euro Info Centre
Société du Centre Méditerranéen de Commerce International (SOMECIN)
2, rue Henri-Barbusse
13241   Marseille cedex 01
France

Contact Mme. Martine LIOGIER
Tel 33 91393377
Fax 33 91393360

Euro Info Centre
Association Euro Info Centre Languedoc-Roussillon
254, rue Michel Teule
ZAC d'Alco – BP 6076
34030   Montpellier cedex 1
France

Contact Mme. Dominique GUY-CHEVANNE
Tel 33 67618151
Fax 33 67618159

Euro Info Centre
Chambre Régionale de Commerce et d'Industrie 'Centre'
35, avenue de Paris
45000   Orléans
France

Contact M. Bernard COTTIN
Tel 33 38545858
Fax 33 38540909

Euro Info Centre Île de France
9a, rue de la Porte de Buc
78021   Versailles
France

Contact Mme. Isabelle DREVET
Tel 33 1 39205854/64
Fax 33 1 39205878

EuroMarketing

Euro Info Centre Centre Français du Commerce Extérieur 10, avenue d'Iéna 75783 Paris France	Contact M. Jean-Michel BALLING Tel 33 1 40733000 Fax 33 1 40733048
Euro Info Centre Ministère de l'Industrie, de la Poste et des Télécommunications 20, avenue de Ségur 75353 Paris 07 SP France	Contact M. Denis LAGNIEZ Tel 33 1 43192816 Fax 33 1 43196037

Euro Info Centre
Chambre de Commerce et
d'Industrie de Paris
Direction des Etudes
27, avenue de Friedland
75382   Paris cedex 08
France
	Contact Mme. Isabelle
	         AMAGLIO-TERISSE
	Tel 33 1 42897313
	Fax 33 1 42897306
	Telex 230 823 DRICCIP
	E-mail fr274_paris@vans.
	         infonet.com

Euro Info Centre Association Poitou-Charentes Europe Immeuble Antarès Avenue du Téléport – BP 110 86960 Poitiers-Futuroscope cedex France	Contact Mme. Laurence MATAS Tel 33 49496330 Fax 33 49490770
Euro Info Centre Bretagne 1, rue du Général Guillaudot 35044 Rennes France	Contact Mlle. Anne DE PUYMALY Tel 33 99254157 Fax 33 99633528

Euro Info Centres

Euro Info Centre de Haute
Normandie
9, rue Robert Schuman
76000   Rouen
France

Contact   M. Christian CHUPIN
Tel   33 35884442
Fax   33 35880652

Euro Info Centre
Chambre de Commerce et
d'Industrie
de la Réunion
5 bis, rue de Paris – BP 120
97463   Saint Denis cedex
France

Contact   Mme. Nathalie
          JORON
Tel   262 922400
Fax   262 922424

Euro Info Centre
(Antenne de FR251-Lyon)
Chambre de Commerce et
d'Industrie
d'Annecy et de Haute-Savoie
2, rue du Lac – BP 2072
74011   Annecy cedex
France

Contact   M. Schay BENICHOU
Tel   33 50337205
Fax   33 50337239

Euro Info Centre
(Antenne de FR268-Marseille)
Chambre de Commerce et
d'Industrie
d'Avignon et de Vaucluse
46, cours Jean Jaurès – BP 158
84008   Avignon
France

Contact   M. Jacques de
          ZELICOURT
Tel   33 90148700
Fax   33 90855678

EuroMarketing

Euro Info Centre	Contact	M. Jean-Philippe
(Antenne de FR251-Lyon)		BONNARD
GREX/Centre de Commerce	Tel	33 76282837/43
International	Fax	33 76282835
Chambre de Commerce et d'Industrie	E-mail	grextp@esc-grenoble.fr
WTC – Grenoble		
5, place Robert Schuman		
38025 Grenoble cedex 1		
France		

Euro Info Centre	Contact	Mme. Anne
(Antenne de FR268-Marseille)		GRAVOULET
C.C.I. Nice Côte d'Azur	Tel	33 93137305/7490
20, boulevard Carabacel	Fax	33 93137474
BP 259		
06005 Nice cedex 1		
France		

Euro Info Centre de Pointe-à-Pitre	Contact	Mlle. Vasanta
Complexe World Trade Center		VENCHARD
Boulevard de la Pointe Jarry	Tel	590 250616/17
97122 Baie-Mahaut	Fax	590 250606
France	E-mail	fr1284-guadeloupe@ vans.infonet.com

Euro Info Centres

Germany

Euro Info Centre
Zenit GmbH
Dohne 54
Postfach 10 22 64
45468   Mülheim an der Ruhr
Germany

Contact   Ms Hannelore
             KRAFT
Tel   49 208 3000421
Fax   49 208 3000429
Telex   20 83 63 ZENITM
E-mail   mk@www.zenit.de

Euro Info Centre
Rationalisierungs-Kuratorium
der Deutschen Wirschaft (RKW)
Heilwigstrasse 33
20249   Hamburg
Germany

Contact   Mr Gerhard MENZ
Tel   49 40 4602087
Fax   49 40 482032

Euro Info Centre
Deutscher Industrie-und
Handelstag-DIHT
Adenauerallee 148
Postfach 1446
53004   Bonn
Germany

Contact   Ms Ellen
             OESTERREICH
Tel   49 228 104621/22
Fax   49 228 104158

Euro Info Centre
Industrie-und Handelskammer
Regensburg
Martin-Luther-Straße 12
Postfach 11 03 55
93016   Regensburg
Germany

Contact   Mr Franz KNOTT
Tel   49 941 56940
Fax   49 941 5694279

EuroMarketing

Euro Info Centre
Zentralverband des Deutschen
Handwerks (ZDH)
Johanniterstraße 1
Postfach 12 02 70
53044   Bonn
Germany

Contact   Mr Klauspeter
          ZANZIG
Tel   49 228 545299/211
Fax   49 228 545205
E-mail   zanzig@zdh.handwerk.de

Euro Info Centre
Handwerkskammer Stuttgart
Heilbronner Straße, 43
Postfach 10 21 55
70017   Stuttgart
Germany

Contact   Mr Jürgen SCHÄFER
Tel   49 711 1657280
Fax   49 711 1657300
E-mail   info@bwht.s.schuttle.de

Euro Info Centre
Industrie- und Handelskammer
zu Aachen
Theaterstraße 6-10
Postfach 6 50
52007   Aachen
Germany

Contact   Mr Frank MALIS
Tel   49 241 44600
Fax   49 241 4460259
Web site   www.aachen.ihk.de
E-mail   info@aachen.ihk.de

Euro Info Centre ERIC Berlin
in der BAO Berlin
Hardenbergstraße 16-18
10623   Berlin
Germany

Contact   Mrs Monika
          SCHULZ-STRELOW
Tel   49 30 31510240/241
Fax   49 30 31510316/154
E-mail   kub@berlin.ihk.de

Euro Info Centre
Deutsches Informationszentrum
für Technische Regeln (DITR)
im DIN e.V.
Burggrafenstraße 6
10787   Berlin
Germany

Contact   Mrs Bärbel
          ZIMMERMANN
Tel   49 30 26012605/2560
Fax   49 30 2628125
E-mail   wiesner@ditr.din.de

Euro Info Centres

Euro Info Centre
Genossenschaftliche EG-Beratungs-
und Informationsgesellschaft
(GEBI) mbH
Rheinweg 67
53129   Bonn
Germany

Contact Mr Ivo-Michael
         ZSCHERLICH
Tel   49 228 237544
Fax   49 228 237548
Web site ourworld.compuserve.
         com/homepages/gebi
E-mail   100772.334@
         compuserve.com

Euro Info Centre
Deutschen Sparkassen- und
Giroverband (DSGV)
Simrockstraße, 4
53113   Bonn
Germany

Contact Mr Heinz BREIER
Tel   49 228 204319/323
Fax   49 228 204725

Euro Info Centre
Axon Technologie Consult GmbH
Hanseatenhof 8
28195   Bremen
Germany

Contact Mr Klaus LENZ
Tel   49 421 175555
Fax   49 421 171686

Euro Info Centre
Industrie- und Handelskammer für
München und Oberbayern
Max-Joseph-Straße 2
80333   Munich
Germany

Contact Mr Michele FUHS
Tel   49 89 5116209
Fax   49 89 5116290
Web site www.muenchen.ihk.de
E-mail   de115_munchen@vans.
         infonet.com

Euro Info Centre
NATI – Niedersächsische Agentur
für Technologietransfer und
Innovation GbmH
Vahrenwalder Straße 7
30165   Hanover
Germany

Contact Ms Christiane
         FRÖCHTLING
Tel   49 511 9357121/2
Fax   49 511 9357439
E-mail   100425.1503@
         compuserve.com

EuroMarketing

Euro Info Centre
Investitionsbank Schleswig-Holstein
Fleethörn 29-31
Postfach 1128
24103   Kiel
Germany

Contact   Mr Ulrich ADOLF
Tel   49 431 9003497/99
Fax   49 431 9003207

Euro Info Centre
Bundesstelle für Außenhandels-
information (BfAI)
Agrippastraße 87/93
Postfach 10 05 22
50445   Cologne
Germany

Contact   Mrs Barbara
            ZIMNIOK
Tel   49 221 2057273/274
Fax   49 221 2057212/262
Web site ourworld.compuserve.
            com/homepages/bfai
E-mail   106035.377@
            compuserve.com

Euro Info Centre
Europäisches Beratungs-Zentrum
der Deutschen Wirtschaft
Gustav-Heinemann-Ufer 84-88
50968   Cologne
Germany

Contact   Ms Jutta
            ZEMKE-HEYL
Tel   49 221 3708621/623
Fax   49 221 3708840
E-mail   100746.2045@
            compuserve.com

Euro Info Centre
Industrie- und Handelskammer
Südlicher Oberrhein
Lotzbeckstraße 31
Postfach 1547
77905   Lahr
Germany

Contact   Ms Petra STECK
Tel   49 78 2127030
Fax   49 78 21270322

Euro Info Centre
Landesgewerbeanstalt Bayern (LGA)
Tillystaße, 2
90431   Nuremberg
Germany

Contact   Mr Edwin SCHMITT
Tel   49 911 6554933
Fax   49 911 6554935
Web site www.lga.de
E-mail   ides@gw.lga.de

Euro Info Centres

Euro Info Centre Saarbrücken
Franz-Josef-Röder-Straße, 9
66119   Saarbrücken
Germany

Contact   Mr Gerd MARTIN
Tel   49 681 9520450
Fax   49 681 5846125
E-mail   101473.3274@
            compuserve.com

Euro Info Centre Rheinland-Pfalz
Bahnhofstraße 30-32
Postfach 1930
54209   Trier
Germany

Contact   Ms Silke
            BRÜGGEBORS
Tel   49 651 1992
Fax   49 651 9756733
E-mail   100567.3225@
            compuserve.com

Euro Info Centre
Wirtschaftsförderung Hessen Investitionsbank AG – HLT
Abraham-Lincoln-Straße 38-42
Postfach 3107
65021   Wiesbaden
Germany

Contact   Mr Volker SCHUCHT
Tel   49 611 774257
Fax   49 611 774385

Euro Info Centre Omnibera (Satellite)
Wirtschaftsberatungsgesellschaft mbH
Coburger Straße 1c
53113   Bonn
Germany

Contact   Mr Michael FEY
Tel   49 228 238078
Fax   49 228 233922

Euro Info Centre
Landesbank Hessen-Thüringen
Bahnhofstraße, 4a
Postfach 167
99004   Erfurt
Germany

Contact   Ms Christine KRATZKE
Tel   49 361 5624798
Fax   49 361 6657233

EuroMarketing

Euro Info Centre
Industrie- und Handelskammer
zu Leipzig
Goerdelerring 5
04091   Leipzig
Germany

Contact   Ms Christa
          FRIEDRICH
Tel   49 341 1267325
Fax   49 341 1267425
Web site   www.diht.infol.ihk.de
E-mail   friedrich@leipzig.ihk.de

Euro Info Centre
Industrie- und Handelskammer
Rostock
Geschäftsbereich EG-Markt und
Außenhandel
Ernst-Barlach-Straße 7
Postfach 10 52 40
18010   Rostock
Germany

Contact   Mr Dieter
          PFLEIGENSDÖRFER
Tel   49 381 338801
Fax   49 381 4591156

Euro Info Centre
Handswerkskammer Magdeburg
Bahnhofstraße 49a
Postfach 15 68
39005   Magdeburg
Germany

Contact   Mr Heinz-Dieter
          DÖMLAND
Tel   49 391 5619161
Fax   49 391 5619162
E-mail   100710.746@
          compuserve.com

Euro Info Centre
Industrie- und Handelskammer
Frankfurt (Oder)
Logenstraße 8
Postfach 343
15203   Frankfurt (Oder)
Germany

Contact   Ms Sabine ANDERS
Tel   49 335 23863/23888
Fax   49 335 322271
E-mail   eic.ihk_ffo@t_online.de

Euro Info Centre
Wirtschaftsförderung Brandenburg
GmbH
Am Lehnitzsee
14476   Neu Fahrland-Potsdam
Germany

Contact   Ms Marzella GERNAND
Tel   49 332 0855224
Fax   49 332 0855222

Euro Info Centres

Euro Info Centre
Industrie- und Handelskammer
Dresden
Niedersedlitzer Straße, 63
01257   Dresden
Germany

Contact   Mr Dieter JÄHNICHEN
Tel   49 351 2802185/186
Fax   49 351 2802280

Euro Info Centre
Fachhochschule Osnabrück
Postfach 19 40
Albrechtstraße 30
49009   Osnabrück
Germany

Contact   Mr Friedrich UHRMACHER
Tel   49 541 9692924
Fax   49 541 9692990
Web site www.et.fh-osnabrueck. de/egbuero/egsurfer. html
E-mail   egbuero@hermes.rz. fh-osnabrueck.de

Euro Info Centre
Industrie- und Handelskammer
Rhein-Neckar
Postfach 10 16 61
68016   Mannheim
Germany

Contact   Ms Petra SCHULZE-SCHWICKING
Tel   49 621 1709227
Fax   49 621 1709219

157

EuroMarketing

Greece

Euro Info Centre
Athens Chamber of Commerce
and Industry
Akadimias Street, 7
10671   Athens
Greece

Contact   Ms Sotiroula
          MOUKAKOU
Tel   30 1 3627337
Fax   30 1 3607897
E-mail   ebea@ermis.acci.
          ariadne-t.gr

Euro Info Centre Eommex
Xenias Street, 16
11528   Athens
Greece

Contact   Ms Evi PANAGIO
          TAKOPOULOU
Tel   30 1 7794229
Fax   30 1 7778694

Euro Info Centre
Federation of Industries
of Northern Greece
Morihovou Square, 1
54625   Thessaloniki
Greece

Contact   Mr Yanis STAVROU
Tel   30 31539817/9682
Fax   30 31541491

Euro Info Centre
Panhellenic Exporters Association
Kratinou, 11
10552   Athens
Greece

Contact   Ms Catherine
          TZORTZINAKI
Tel   30 1 5228925
Fax   30 1 5242568
E-mail   eicpea@compulink.gr

Euro Info Centre
Chamber of Commerce and
Industry of Iraklion
Koronaeou Street, 9
71202 Iraklion, Crete
Greece

Contact   Ms Maria PETRAKI
Tel   30 81 285829
Fax   30 81 225730

Euro Info Centre
Chamber of Kavala
Omonias Street, 50
65302   Kavala
Greece

Contact   Ms Soultana
          MAVROMMATI
Tel   30 51 833964
Fax   30 52 835946
E-mail   gr1157_kavala@vans.
          infonet.com

Euro Info Centres

Euro Info Centre Eommex
Hellenic Organization of Small and
Medium Sized Industries and
Handicrafts
Marinou Antipa & Kouma Street
41222   Larissa
Greece

Contact   Mr Sotiris BLANAS
Tel   30 41 226077
Fax   30 41 253019

Euro Info Centre Eommex
Hellenic Organization of Small and
Medium Sized Industries and
Handicrafts
Aratou Street, 21
26221   Patras
Greece

Contact   Ms Georgia
              GIOVRIE-SKODRA
Tel   30 61 220248
Fax   30 61 223496

Euro Info Centre
Chamber of Commerce and
Industry
Loudovicou Street, 1
Place Odissou
18531   Piraeus
Greece

Contact   Mr George
              DROUBOUKIS
Tel   30 1 4170529
Fax   30 1 4174601

Euro Info Centre
Association of Industries in
Thessaly and in Central Greece
E1. Venizelou Rd, 4
38221   Volos
Greece

Contact   Mrs Stella VAINA
Tel   30 421 28111/29407
Fax   30 421 26394

Euro Info Centre
Chamber of Commerce of Ioannina
X.Trikoupi & O.Poutetsi
Str.14
45332   Ioannina
Greece

Contact   Mr Yannis
              DASKALOPOULOS
Tel   30 651 76589
Fax   30 651 25179

EuroMarketing

Iceland

Euro Info Centre
Trade Council of Iceland
Hallveigarstig, 1
PO Box 1000
121   Reykjavik
Iceland

Contact   Mr Andrés
          PETURSSON
Tel   354 5114000
Fax   354 5114040
Web site www.icetrade.is
E-mail   euroinfo@icetrade.is

Euro Info Centres

Ireland

Euro Info Centre
Irish Trade Board/An Bord
Trachtala
Merrion Hall
Strand Road, Sandymount
Dublin 4
Ireland

Contact Ms Margaret HOGAN
Tel 353 1 2066000
Fax 353 1 2066367

Euro Info Centre
Shannon Development
The Granary
Michael Street
Limerick
Ireland

Contact Ms Nuala O'CARROLL
Tel 353 61 410777
Fax 353 61 315634
E-mail ocarrol@shannon-dev.ie

Euro Info Centre
Cork Chamber of Commerce
67/69 South Mall
Cork
Ireland

Contact Mrs Tara DENNEHY
Tel 353 21 509044
Fax 353 21 271347
Web site www.eirenet.net/ccc/eic/
E-mail eic@corkchamber.iol.ie

Euro Info Centre
Galway Chamber of Commerce
and Industry
Commerce House
Merchants Road
Galway
Ireland

Contact Ms Adrienne HARTEN
Tel 353 91 562624
Fax 353 91 561963
E-mail comgal@iol.ie

Euro Info Centre
Sligo Chamber of Commerce
and Industry
16 Quay Street
Sligo
Ireland

Contact Mr Brian CARTY
Tel 353 71 61274
Fax 353 71 60912

EuroMarketing

Euro Info Centre	Contact	Ms Julie O'ROURKE
Waterford Chamber of Commerce	Tel	353 51 72639
CTT Office Industrial Estate	Fax	353 51 79220
Cork Road	Telex	80 273
Waterford		
Ireland		

Italy

Euro Info Centre Azienda Speciale-
Camera di Commercio
Industria Artigianato e Agricoltura
di Milano
Via Ansperto, 5
20123   Milan
Italy

Contact   Mr Attilio
          MARTINETTI
Tel   39 2 85155243/5244
Fax   39 2 85155308
Web site www.mi.camcom.it/
          eurosportello
E-mail   eic@mi.camcom.it

Euro Info Centre
Camera di Commercio Industria
Artigianato e Agricoltura di Napoli
Corso Meridionale, 58
80143   Naples
Italy

Contact   Mr Riccardo
          DE FALCO
Tel   39 81 5536106/
          284217
Fax   39 81 287675

Euro Info Centre
Rete Artigianato
Via Giovanni Bruni, 17
25121   Brescia
Italy

Contact   Ms Brunella SCALVINI
Tel   39 30 3774770/75
Fax   39 30 3774812

Euro Info Centre
Confindustria – Direzione PMI
Viale dell'Astronomia, 30
00144   Rome
Italy

Contact   Mr Guiseppe VOLPE
Tel   39 6 5903613/352
Fax   39 6 5903291/
          5910629

Euro Info Centre
Associazione degli Industriali
della Provincia di Bologna
Via San Domenico, 4
40124   Bologna
Italy

Contact   Mr Andrea
          DALLEDONNE
Tel   39 51 529611
Fax   39 51 529613
E-mail   assindustria-bo@bo-
          nettuno.it

EuroMarketing

Euro Info Centre
Camera di Commercio Industria
Artigianato e Agricoltura di Ascoli
Piceno
Via L. Mercantini, 23/25
63100   Ascoli Piceno
Italy

Contact   Mr Francesco
DI MATTEO
Tel   39 736 279203/233
Fax   39 736 262144
Web site www.topnet.it/provinci/homeap.htm
E-mail   it/356_ascolipiceno@vans.infonet.com

Euro Info Centre
Istituto Finanziario Regionale
Pugliese (Finpuglia)
Via Lenin, 2
777-125   Bari
Italy

Contact   Ms Alessandra
DE LUCA
Tel   39 80 5016735/890
Fax   39 80 5016809

Euro Info Centre
Camera di Commercio Industria
Artigianato e Agricoltura Cagliari
Viale Diaz, 221
c/o Centro Servizi
09126   Cagliari
Italy

Contact   Mr Giulio LECCA
Tel   39 70 306877/308977
Fax   39 70 340328

Euro Info Centre
Camera di Commercio Industria
Artigianato e Agricoltura di Catania
Salita Cappuccini, 2
95124   Catania
Italy

Contact   Mr Giuseppe LANTERI
Tel   39 95 7150176
Fax   39 95 7150265

Euro Info Centre Promofirenze
Orcagna 68-70
50121   Florence
Italy

Contact   Mr Santi SEMPLICI
Tel   39 55 280132
Fax   39 55 283304

Euro Info Centres

Euro Info Centre Confesercenti Consorzio Eurosportello Confesercenti Piazza E.Artom, 12 50127 Florence Italy	Contact Tel Fax Web site E-mail	Mr Lucio SCOGNAMIGLIO 39 55 4393395/402 39 55 4393391 www.confesercenti.it/ eic.htm eic_it362@confes ercenti.it
Euro Info Centre Liguria Torre World Trade Center Via de Marini, 1 16149 Genoa Italy	Contact Tel Fax E-mail	Miss Raffaella BRUZZONE 39 10 2094252/434 39 10 2094297 euroinfo@relay.ge. camcom.it
Euro Info Centre Assolombarda Via Pantamo, 9 20122 Milan Italy	Contact Tel Fax E-mail	Mr Luigi BOLDRIN 392 58370382/411/459 392 58370416 oro133@ibm.net
Euro Info Centre Centro Estero Umbria Camera di Commercio di Perugia Via Cacciatori delle Alpi, 42 06100 Perugia Italy	Contact Tel Fax	Mr Fulvio OCCHIUCCI 39 75 5748206/21852 39 75 5728088
Euro Info Centre Associazione 'Compagnia delle Opere' Via Rossi, 2 61100 Pesaro Italy	Contact Tel Fax	Mr Stephano FABBRINI 39 721 410088 39 721 414174

EuroMarketing

Euro Info Centre Azienda Speciale 'Sportello di Informazione e Documentazione per le Imprese' Viale L.C. Farini, 14 48100 Ravenna Italy	Contact Mr Antonio NANNINI Tel 39 544 481417 Fax 39 544 218731 E-mail eicit369ra@provincia. ravenna.it
Euro Info Centre Confederazione Generale dell'Agricoltura Italiana Corso Vittorio Emanuele II, 101 00186 Rome Italy	Contact Mr Filippo TRIFILETTI Tel 39 6 6852378 Fax 39 6 6861726

Euro Info Centre
Confederazione Generale Italiana
del Commercio e del Turismo
Piazza G. Gioacchino Belli, 2
00153   Rome
Italy
	Contact Mrs Maria Rita
	                 MASCI
	Tel 39 6 5898973/
	                 5897613
	Fax 39 6 5814984

Euro Info Centre Istituto per la Promozione Industriale (IPI) Viale Maresciallo Pilsudski, 124 00197 Rome Italy	Contact Mr Valentino BOLIC Tel 39 6 80972210/3/6/9 Fax 39 6 80972212
Euro Info Centre ICE-Veronafiere Istituto Nazionale per il Commercio Estero (ICE) Viale del Lavoro, 8 37135 Verona Italy	Contact Mrs Ida OSSI Tel 39 45 8293911/8283 Fax 39 45 8298245 E-mail euroinfo@eurosportell ovr.inet.it

Euro Info Centres

Euro Info Centre
Unioncamere-Mondimpresa-Cerved
Piazza Sallustio, 21
00187   Rome
Italy

Contact   Mrs Monica DIDO
Tel   39 6 47041/4704206
Fax   39 6 4704342

Euro Info Centre
Camera di Commercio Industria
Artigianato e Agricoltura di Torino
Via San Francesco da Paola, 24
10123   Turin
Italy

Contact   Mr Riccardo RICOTTA
Tel   39 11 5716370
Fax   39 11 5716517
E-mail   eurosportello@st.alpcom.it

Euro Info Centre
Federazione delle Associazioni
Industriali del Piemonte
(Federpiemonte)
Corso Stati Uniti, 38
10128   Turin
Italy

Contact   Mr Ermanno MARITANO
Tel   39 11 549246
Fax   39 11 5175204

Euro Info Centre
Centro Friulano per il Commercio
Estero
Division C.C.I.A.A. Servizi srl
Viale Ungheria, 15
33100   Udine
Italy

Contact   Ms Laura TREVISAN
Tel   39 432 248826/7/8
Fax   39 432 503919

Euro Info Centre Veneto
Centro Estero delle Camere di
Commercio del Veneto
Via G. Pepe, 104
30172   Venice Mestre
Italy

Contact   Mr Gian Angelo BELLATI
Tel   39 41 988200
Fax   39 41 989548
E-mail   itl378_veneto@vans.infonet.com

EuroMarketing

Euro Info Centre
Associazione Industriali della
Provincia di Vicenza
Piazza Castello, 3
36100   Vicenza
Italy

Contact   Mr Lorenzo MAGGIO
Tel   39 444 232580
Fax   39 444 232686

Euro Info Centre
Mondimpresa/Unioncamere Sicilia
Confindustria Sicilia
Via Emerico Amari, 11
90139   Palermo
Italy

Contact   Mr Claudio LEONE
Tel   39 91 321510
Fax   39 91 321703

Luxembourg

Euro Info Centre
Chambre de Commerce du
Grand-Duché
de Luxembourg/FEDIL
Rue Alcide de Gasperi, 7
B.P. 1503
2981   Luxembourg
Luxembourg

Contact   Mlle. Sabrina
          SAGRAMOLA
Tel   352 423939333
Fax   352 438326

Euro Info Centre
Chambre des Métiers du
Grand-Duché
de Luxembourg
Circuit de la Foire
Internationale, 2
B.P. 1604
1016   Luxembourg
Luxembourg

Contact   Mlle. Danièle MENSTER
Tel   352 4267671
Fax   352 426787
E-mail   daniele.menster@batel.lu

EuroMarketing

The Netherlands

Euro Info Centre
Kamer van Koophandel en
Fabrieken
voor Amsterdam
De Ruyterkade 5
PO Box 2852
1000 CW   Amsterdam
The Netherlands

Contact　Mr Reinier
　　　　　DE KONING
Tel　　　31 20 5236706
Fax　　　31 20 5236732

Euro Info Centre
Stichting EG-adviescentrum
Zuid-Nederland
PO Box 70060
Pettelaarpark, 10
5201 DZ   's-Hertogenbosch
The Netherlands

Contact　Mr Hans ABEN
Tel　　　31 73 6806600
Fax　　　31 73 6123210
E-mail　egadvies@pi.net

Euro Info Centre Nederland
EVD EG-Liaison
Postbus 20105
Bezuidenhoutseweg, 151
2500 EC   den Haag
The Netherlands

Contact　Mr Hans VLOT
Tel　　　31 70 3798811
Fax　　　31 70 3797878

Euro Info Centre Noord-Nederland
Stichting Euro Info Centrum
Noord-Nederland
Damsport, 1
PO Box 424
9700 AK   Groningen
The Netherlands

Contact　Mr Wim
　　　　　VAN DRUENEN
Tel　　　31 50 5214470
Fax　　　31 50 5214400
E-mail　nvnom@noord.bart.nl

Euro Info Centres

Euro Info Centre Oost-Nederland
Stichting Euro Info Centrum
Gelderland
Kerkenbos 10-02
Postbus 383261
6503 AH   Nijmegen
The Netherlands

Contact   Mr Guus SCHEEPERS
Tel   31 24 3780075
Fax   31 24 3777029
E-mail   eic457@tref.nl

Euro Info Centre Midden-
Nederland
St. Jacobsstraat, 16
PO Box 48
3500 AA   Utrecht
The Netherlands

Contact   Mrs Karin
             KERCKHAERT
Tel   31 30 2368457
Fax   31 30 2368541
E-mail   eicmn@worldaccess.nl

Euro Info Centre
Stichting Euro Info Centrum
Zuid-Holland
Stationsweg 41
PO Box 2059
2301 CB   Leiden
The Netherlands

Contact   Ms Milëne TROMP
Tel   31 71 5146101
Fax   31 71 5142568

EuroMarketing

Norway

Euro Info Centre
The Norwegian Trade Council
Drammensveien, 40
0243   Oslo
Norway

Contact Mr Hans J. GROLL
Tel   47 22926570
Fax   47 22431640
E-mail   euroinfo@ntc.geis.com

Euro Info Centre
VINN-North Norwegian Institute
of Technology and Innovation
Teknologiveien, 10
PO Box 253
8501   Narvik
Norway

Contact   Ms Ingrid
          MARTENSON
Tel   47 76922222
Fax   47 76947260
Web site www.vinn.no/
E-mail   eicnord@vinn.no

Euro Info Centre
Vestlandsforsking
(Western Norway Research Institute)
Fossetunet, 3
PO Box 163
5801   Sogndal
Norway

Contact Mr Terje AABERGE
Tel   47 57676050
Fax   47 57676190
E-mail   taa@vf.hisf.no

Euro Info Centre
Agderforsking
Tordenskjoldsgate, 65
PO Box 2074   Posebyen
4611   Kristiansand
Norway

Contact Ms Maj-Britt HAVER
Tel   47 38025055
Fax   47 38025090
E-mail   eicsor@agderforskning.
         no

Euro Info Centre Mid Norway
Sør-Trøndelag Næringsservice
Sluppenveien, 12E
PO Box 6018
7003   Trondheim
Norway

Contact Ms Lisbeth VASSAAS
Tel   47 73962230
Fax   47 73962218
E-mail   soer@telepost.no

Portugal

Euro Info Centre
Associação Industrial Portuense
Exponor P-4450
Leça da Palmeira (Porto)
Portugal

Contact   Mrs Maria Helena
           RAMOS
Tel   351 2 9981580
Fax   351 2 9957017
E-mail   eurog@telepac.pt

Euro Info Centre
Banco de Fomento e Exterior
Av. Casal Ribeiro, 59
1000   Lisbon
Portugal

Contact   Mr Manuel LINO
Tel   351 1 3560144
Fax   351 1 3431728
Web site www://grupo.bfe.pt
E-mail   lelia_de_jesus@office.
            bfe.pt

Euro Info Centre
Associação Industrial do Distrito
de Aveiro
Cais da Fonte Nova (Antigo Edif.
Fáb. Jeronimo P. Campos
Alçado Sul-3° Piso
3800   Aveiro
Portugal

Contact   Mr José de
           MATOS RODRIGUES
Tel   351 34 20095
Fax   351 34 24093
E-mail   aida@mail.telepac.pt

Euro Info Centre Região Centro
Comissão de Coordenacão da
Região Centro
Rua Luis de Camoes, 150
3000   Coimbra
Portugal

Contact   Miss Alda Maria
           DOS SANTOS REIS
Tel   351 39 701475/
           701562
Fax   351 39 405688
Web site www.ccr-c.pt./acores/
            eurogabinete
E-mail   eicrc@mail.telepac.pt

Euro Info Centre PME
Instituto de Apoio às
Pequenas e Médias Empresas e ao
Investimento
Rua de Valasco, 19 C
7000   Évora
Portugal

Contact   Mr António MOURATO
Tel   351 66 21875/6
Fax   351 66 29781
E-mail   pt1505_iapme@vans.
            infonet.com

EuroMarketing

Euro Info Centre
Commissão de Coordenação da
Região do Algarve
Praça da Liberdade, 2
8000   Faro
Portugal

Contact   Mr João GUERREIRO
Tel   351 89 802709
Fax   351 89 806687
E-mail   euroalgarve@mail.telepac.pt

Euro Info Centre Madeira
Avenida Arriaga, 41
9000   Funchal
Portugal

Contact   Mr Rui JERVIS
Tel   351 91 230137
Fax   351 91 222005

Euro Info Centre
Associação Industrial Portuguesa
Praça das Indústrias
Apartado 3200
1301   Lisbon
Portugal

Contact   Mrs Silvina BAPTISTA
Tel   351 1 3639458
Fax   351 1 3646786
E-mail   date@mail.telepac.pt

Euro Info Centre/Eurogabinete
Caixa Geral de Depósitos
Avenida João XXI
63-5° Andar
1000   Lisbon
Portugal

Contact   Mrs Maria Sofia LOPO
Tel   351 1 7905389
Fax   351 1 7905097
Web site   www//euroinfo.ce.pt
E-mail   pt1509_lisboa@vans.infonet.com

Euro Info Centre
Câmara do Comércio e Indústria
dos Açores
Rua Ernesto do Canto, 13
9500   Ponta Delgada
Portugal

Contact   Mr José Manuel MONTEIRO DA SILVA
Tel   351 96 23235/22427
Fax   351 96 24268
E-mail   eurogab.acores@telepac.pt

Euro Info Centres

Euro Info Centre (Satellite of	Contact	Ms Paula Cr.
PT504-Coimbra)		MATOS NUNES
Associacão Comercial e Industrial	Tel	351 39 492402
de Coimbra (A.C.I.C.)	Fax	351 39 492064
Parque de Feiras e Exposições
Alto da Relvinha
3020   Coimbra
Portugal

Euro Info Centre (Satellite of	Contact	Mrs Roselene
PT510-Ponta Delgada)		DORES
Câmara do Comércio de Angra do	Tel	351 95 23470
Heroísmo	Fax	351 95 27131
Rua da Palha, 32/34
9700   Angra do Heroismo
Portugal

EuroMarketing

Spain

Euro Info Centre
CIDEM/FTN
Av. Diagonal, 403 1r-
08008   Barcelona
Spain

Contact   Mr Xavier CASARES
          MARTINEZ
Tel   34 3 4151114
Fax   34 3 2186747
Web site www.gencat.es/cidem
E-mail   cideminfo@cinet.fcn.es

Euro Info Centre
Cámara de Comercio,
Industria y Navegación de Bilbao
Alameda de Recalde, 50
48008   Bilbao (Bizkaia)
Spain

Contact   Mr Enrique VELASCO-
          RUIZ DE OLALLA
Tel   34 4 4104503
Fax   34 4 4446324
E-mail   es1202_bilbao@vans.
          infonet.com

Euro Info Centre
Confederación de Empresarios
de Andalucía
Isla de la Cartuja, s/n
41010   Seville
Spain

Contact   Mme. Mercedes
          LEON LOZANO
Tel   34 5 4460001
Fax   34 5 4461644

Euro Info Centre
Confederación Española de
Organisaciones
Empresariales
Diego de León, 50
28006   Madrid
Spain

Contact   Mme. Carmen
          GARCIA COSSIO
Tel   34 1 5639641
Fax   34 1 5640135

Euro Info Centre
Centro Europeo de Información
Empresarial ICEX-IMPI
Paseo de la Castellana, 14
28046   Madrid
Spain

Contact   Mme. Ana Isabel
          ARECES ESTRADA
Tel   34 1 3491831
Fax   34 1 5750025

Euro Info Centres

Euro Info Centre
Confederación Regional de
Empresarios
de Castilla la Mancha
Calle Rosario, 29
02001   Albacete
Spain

Contact   Mme. Victoria LOPEZ
          VALCARCEL
Tel   34 67 217300/01/04
Fax   34 67 240202/212149

Euro Info Centre Argentaria-BEX
Banco Exterior de España
Paseo de Gracia, 25
08007   Barcelona
Spain

Contact   M. Jorge GARCIA
          GALCERAN
Tel   34 3 4822970/71/72
Fax   34 3 4822974
E-mail   es1208_bex@vans.
          infonet.com

Euro Info Centre
Cámara Oficial de Comercio,
Industria y Navegación
Avenida Diagonal, 452–454
08006   Barcelona
Spain

Contact   M. Rafael GARCIA
          SANTOS
Tel   34 3 4169389
Fax   34 3 4160735

Euro Info Centre
Ayuntamiento de Cáceres
Edificio 'la Chicuela'
c/o Sánchez Herrero, 2
10004   Cáceres
Spain

Contact   Mme. Rebeca
          DOMINGUEZ-
          CIDONCHA
Tel   34 27 217183
Fax   34 27 217059

Euro Info Centre de Navarra
San Cosme y San Damían, s/n
31191   Cordovilla – Pamplona
Spain

Contact   Mrs Mae HERIAS
           OSCARIZ
Tel   34 48 421101
Fax   34 48 421100
Web site   www.ain.es
E-mail   ain@pna.servicom.es

EuroMarketing

Euro Info Centre
Gobierno de Canarias
Conserjería de Economía y
Hacienda
C/Nicolás Estévanez, 33
35007   Las Palmas de G. Canaria
Spain

Contact   Ms Maria DIAZ-
          CASANOVA SUAREZ
Tel   34 28 271142
Fax   34 28 275144/227812

Euro Info Centre
Federación de Empresarios de
la Rioja
Calle Hermanos Moroy, 8 – 4°
26001   Logroño
Spain

Contact   Mrs Monica
          BARTOLOME OSINAGA
Tel   34 41 257022
Fax   34 41 262537

Euro Info Centre
Cámara de Comercio e Industria
de Madrid
Plaza de la Independencia, 1
28001   Madrid
Spain

Contact   Mrs Carmen
          VERDERA
Tel   34 1 5383610
Fax   34 1 5383643

Euro Info Centre IMADE
Centro Europeo de Información
Empresarial
Gran Via, 42
28013   Madrid
Spain

Contact   Mrs Ines COLLADO
          NAVARRO
Tel   34 1 5802600
Fax   34 1 5802589

Euro Info Centre
Proyecto Europa – Banesto
Centro Europeo de Información
Plaza de la Constitución, 9
29008   Málaga
Spain

Contact   Miss Nuria TOUCET
          ALVAREZ
Tel   34 5 2220959
Fax   34 5 2220936

Euro Info Centres

Euro Info Centre
Instituto de Fomento de la Región
de Murcia
Plaza San Agustín, 5
30005   Murcia
Spain

Contact Mrs Maria Jesus
         CACHORRO
         SANCHEZ
Tel   34 68 362818
Fax   34 68 293245
E-mail   es1217_murcia@vans.
         infonet.com

Euro Info Centre
Instituto de Fomento Regional
Parque Tecnológico de Asturias
33420   Llanera
Spain

Contact Mr Rosendo ROJAS
         SANCHEZ
Tel   34 85 260068
Fax   34 85 264455
E-mail   ifr@asturnet.es

Euro Info Centre
Centro Balears Europa
Calle Ramon Llull, 2
Edificio Sa Nostra
07001   Palma de Mallorca
Spain

Contact   Mrs Grace GARCIA
          SANTOS
Tel   34 71 717374
Fax   34 71 714681
Web site www.bitel.es/cbe
E-mail   cbe@bitel.es

Euro Info Centre
Fundación Euroventanilla
del País Vasco
C/Tomas Gros, 3 bajo
20001   Donostia San Sebastián
Spain

Contact Mr Pedro PALOMO
Tel   34 43 272288
Fax   34 43 271657
E-mail   fundac04@sarenet.es

Euro Info Centre
Confederación de Empresarios
de Galicia
Rúa do Vilar, 54
15705   Santiago de Compostela
Spain

Contact Ms Maria Esther
         PEREIRAS NEIRA
Tel   34 81 560699
Fax   34 81 565788
E-mail   casaga@ibm.net

EuroMarketing

Euro Info Centre	Contact	Mr Javier DIAZ
Toleda-Castilla la Mancha		HERRANZ
Plaza San Vicente, 3	Tel	34 25 214450
45001 Toledo	Fax	34 25 213900
Spain		

Euro Info Centre	Contact	Mr Vicente MOMPO
Cámara Oficial de Comercio,	Tel	34 6 3511301
Industria y Navegación de Valencia	Fax	34 6 3516349
C/Poeta Querol, 15		
46002 Valencia		
Spain		

Euro Info Centre	Contact	Mrs Carolina CALVO
Sodical		REVILLA
C/Claudio Moyano, 4 – 1°	Tel	34 83 354033
47001 Valladolid	Fax	34 83 354738
Spain		

Euro Info Centre	Contact	Mr Jorge ALONSO
Confederación Regional de		VALLEJO
Empresarios de Aragón	Tel	34 76 320000
Plaza Roma F-1, la planta	Fax	34 76 322956
50010 Zaragoza	E-mail	creaeic@mail.
Spain		sendanet.es

Euro Info Centre (Antenne de	Contact	Mrs Maria MARTIN
ES218-Llanera)	Tel	34 8 5232105
Federación Asturiana de	Fax	34 8 5244176
Empresarios F.A.D.E.	E-mail	empres@ibm.net
c/ Dr. Alfredo Martinez, 6-2a planta		
33005 Oviedo		
Spain		

Euro Info Centres

Sweden

Euro Info Centre Nutek
Liljeholmsvägen, 32
117 86   Stockholm
Development
Sweden

Contact   Ms Maria OLOFSSON
Tel   46 868191
Fax   46 87444045
Web site www.nutek.se
E-mail   eic@nutek.se

Euro Info Centre SYD
IDEON Science Park
PA Hanssons väg, 43B
205 12   Malmö
Sweden

Contact   Mr Bjarne MEYER
Tel   46 40321032
Fax   46 40321033
Web site www.euroinfo.se/
E-mail   anders.krantz@
              euroinfo.se

Euro Info Centre – Mälar region
Europa Instituteti Västerås
Stora Gatan, 16
722 12   Västerås
Sweden

Contact   Ms Maria GUSTAFSON
Tel   46 21107860
Fax   46 21107869
Web site www.euroinfo.se
E-mail   c.tegerstrand@arosnet.
              se

Euro Info Centre
Företagarnas Riksorganisation
(Federation of Private Enterprises)
Ölandsgatan, 6
PO Box 1958
791 19   Falun
Sweden

Contact   Ms Madeleine NEIL
Tel   46 2358130
Fax   46 2358156
E-mail   madeleine.neil@falun.
              euroinfo.se

Euro Info Centre East & Central
Sweden
Östsvenska Europakontoret (ÖEK)
Almi Företagspartner Örebro AB
(ALMI)
Nya Rådstugugatan, 3
602 24   Norrköping
Sweden

Contact   Mr Jan OLOFSSON
Tel   46 1112119
Fax   46 11137719
E-mail   euroinfo.east@os
              teurokont.se

EuroMarketing

Euro Info Centre Sydost
Almi Företagspartner Kronoberg AB
Västra Esplanaden, 5
PO Box 1501
351 15   Växjö
Sweden

Contact   Ms Ulla ROLF
Tel   46 47023044
Fax   46 47027937
E-mail   eic.sydost@almi.se

Euro Info Centre West Sweden
Trade and Industry Development
Agency in Göteborg
Norra Hamngatan, 14
411 14   Göteborg
Sweden

Contact   Mr Lars EKBERG
Tel   46 31612418
Fax   46 31612401
E-mail   ingrid_gunnarsson@
westsweden.se

Euro Info Centre Stockholm AB
Box 12712
Hantverkargatan, 2F
112 94   Stockholm
Sweden

Contact   Mr. Christer DAHLBERG
Tel   46 867858050
Fax   46 86500119

Euro Info Centre
Jönköping Chamber of Commerce
Elmiavägen
554 54   Jönköping
Sweden

Contact Mr Carl-Gustaf
           BJÖRSTRAND
Tel   46 36127001
Fax   46 36129579
Web site www.ltc.se
E-mail   anders@jn.wtc.se

Euro Info Centres

United Kingdom

Euro Info Centre Limited
Scottish Enterprise
21 Bothwell Street
G2 6NL Glasgow
UK

Contact Mr Ian TRAILL
Tel   44 141 2210999
Fax   44 141 2216539
E-mail   lesley.magaire@scotnet.co.uk

Euro Info Centre
Birmingham Chamber of Commerce and Industry
75 Harborne Road
B15 3DH   Birmingham
UK

Contact Miss Cathy DAVIES
Tel   44 121 4550268
Fax   44 121 4558670

Euro Info Centre
Northern Development Company
Great North House
Sandyford Road
NE1 8ND   Newcastle upon Tyne
UK

Contact Ms Marion SCHOOLER
Tel   44 191 2610026/5131
Fax   44 191 2221774
E-mail   gb1553_newcastle@vans.infonet.com

Euro Info Centre
Local Enterprise Development Unit (L.E.D.U.)
Ledu House
Upper Galwally
BT8 4TB   Belfast
UK

Contact Ms Eleanor BUTTERWICK
Tel   44 1232 491031
Fax   44 1232 691432

Euro Info Centre Sussex
Greenacre Court, Station Road,
RH15 9DS
Burgess Hill (West Sussex)
UK

Contact Miss Vivienne GRAY
Tel   44 1444 259232
Fax   44 1444 259190
E-mail   SCCTE.@pawilicn.com

EuroMarketing

Euro Info Centre
Bristol Chamber of Commerce
and Industry
16 Clifton Park
BS8 3BY   Bristol
UK

Contact   Mrs Sarah HARRIS
Tel   44 117 9737373
Fax   44 117 9745365
E-mail   eic.@blw.westec.co.uk

Euro Info Centre Southwest
Exeter Enterprises
Reed Hall
University of Exeter
EX4 4QR   Exeter
UK

Contact   Ms Christine YOUNG
Tel   44 1392 214085
Fax   44 1392 264375
E-mail   c.young@exeter.ac.uk

Euro Info Centre
Business Information Source
Highland Opportunity Ltd
20 Bridge Street
IV1 1QR   Inverness
UK

Contact   Ms Caroline
           GRAY-STEPHENS
Tel   44 1463 715400
Fax   44 1463 715600
E-mail   eic@sprite.co.uk

Euro Info Centre Humberside
(Satellite of UK571-Bradford)
The University of Hull
Brynmor Jones Library
HU6 7RX   Hull
UK

Contact   Miss Susan ARUNDALE
Tel   44 1482 465940/35
Fax   44 1482 466488
E-mail   s.arundale@lib.hull.ac.
           uk

Euro Info Centre
Leicester European Information
Centre
The Business Centre
10 York Road
LE1 5TS   Leicester
UK

Contact   Ms Rita KOTECHA
Tel   44 116 2559944
Fax   44 116 2553470

Euro Info Centres

Euro Info Centre North West L.A.D.S.I.R.L.A.C. Liverpool Central Libraries William Brown Street L3 8EW Liverpool UK	Contact Mr Howard PATTERSON Tel 44 151 2981928 Fax 44 151 2071342 Web site www.connect.org.uk/merseyworld/eic E-mail info@eicnw.u-net.com.uk
Euro Info Centre Kent County Council Springfield ME14 2LL Maidstone, Kent UK	Contact Mr David OXLADE Tel 44 1622 694109 Fax 44 1622 691418 Web site spectrum.tcns.co.uk/kenteuro/welcome.html E-mail ecdido@tcns.co.uk
Manchester Euro Info Centre Business Link Manchester Churchgate House 56 Oxford Street M60 7BL Manchester UK	Contact Mr Steve CARROLL Tel 44 161 2374020 Fax 44 161 2369945
Euro Info Centre East Anglia Norfolk and Waveney Chamber of Commerce and Industry 112 Barrack Street NR3 1UB Norwich UK	Contact Ms Sarah Jane ABERCROMBIE Tel 44 1603 625977 Fax 44 1603 633032 E-mail euro-info@netcom.co.uk
Euro Info Centre Nottingham Chamber of Commerce and Industry 309 Haydn Road NG5 1DG Nottingham UK	Contact Mr Graham BIRKETT Tel 44 115 9624624 Fax 44 115 9856612

EuroMarketing

Wales Euro Info Centre
Welsh Development Agency
UWCC Guest Building
P.O. Box 430
CF1 3XT   Cardiff
UK

Contact   Mr Brian MEREDITH
Tel   44 1222 229525
Fax   44 1222 229740
Web site www.cityscape.co.uk/
            users/cw63
E-mail   cw63@cityscape.co.uk

Euro Info Centre
Thames Valley Chamber of
Commerce and Industry
Commerce House
2-6 Bath Road
SL1 3SB   Slough
UK

Contact   Ms Anne WHITE
Tel   44 1753 577877
Fax   44 1753 524644

Shropshire and Staffordshire
Euro Info Centre
Trevithick House
Stafford Park 4
TF3 3BA   Telford
UK

Contact   Mrs Susan JOHNSON
Tel   44 1952 208213/228
Fax   44 1952 208208
Web site www.cityscape.co.uk/
            users/gv20
E-mail   ebc_sshire@blink_
            sshire.cityscape.co.uk

Euro Info Centre
Southern Area EIC Consortium
Civic Centre
SO14 7LW   Southampton
UK

Contact   Mr David Anthony
            DANCE
Tel   44 1703 832866
Fax   44 1703 231714
E-mail   xeicsenq@hants.gov.uk

West Yorkshire Euro Info Centre
4 Manchester Road
Mercury House – 2nd Floor
BD5 0QL   Bradford
UK

Contact   Ms Jenny LAWSON
Tel   44 1274 754262
Fax   44 1274 393226
E-mail   jenny@wyebic.demon.
            co.uk

Euro Info Centres

Euro Info Centre
(Satellite of UK569-Telford)
Staffordshire European Business Centre
Business Innovation Centre
Staffordshire Technology Park
Beaconside
ST18 0AR   Stafford
UK

Contact   Ms Jenny THOMAS
Tel   44 1785 222300/ 59528
Fax   44 1785 253207

Euro Info Centre
London Chamber of Commerce and Industry
33 Queen Street
EC4R 1AP   London
UK

Contact   Ms Beth RAYNEY CUCALA
Tel   44 171 489 1992
Fax   44 171 489 0391

Euro Info Centre Westminster
Mitre House
177 Regent Street
London
W1R 8D7
UK

Contact   Ms Beth RAYNEY CUCALA
Tel   44 171 734 6406
Fax   44 171 734 0670
E-mail   tony@naslem.win_uk.net

EURO INFO CENTRES: OUTSIDE THE EUROPEAN UNION

Euro Info Correspondence Centre
Union for Private Economic Enterprise
54 Dr G M Dimitrov Blvd Business Centre – 4th floor
1125   Sofia
Bulgaria

Contact Ms Antonina STOYANOVSKA
Tel 359 2 738448
Fax 359 2 730435
E-mail eicc@cit.sf.bg

Cyprus Euro Info Correspondence Centre
Cyprus Chamber of Commerce and Industry
38 Grivas Dhigenis Avenue
1066   Nicosia
Cyprus

Contact Mrs Elena CHRISTOFIDES-GEORGHIOU
Tel 357 2449500
Fax 357 2361044
E-mail cy1691_eic_cyprus@vans.infonet.com

Euro Info Correspondence Centre
National Information Centre of the Czech Republic (NIS)
Havelkova 22
130 00   Prague 3
Czech Republic

Contact Mrs Marie PAVLU
Czechia
Tel 42 2 24231486
Fax 42 2 24231114
Web site www.dec.nis.cz
E-mail nlpavlu@dec.nis.cz

Euro Info Centres

Euro Info Correspondence Centre
Estonian Chamber of Commerce
and Industry
Toom-Kooli 17
0001   Tallinn 372
Estonia

Contact Mr Erki KOIV
Tel   372 6 460244
Fax   372 6 460245
Web site www.ktk.uninet.ee/eik
E-mail   einfo@ktk.uninet.ee

Euro Info Correspondence Centre
Investment and Trade Development
Agency in Hungary – ITDH
V Dorottya U 4
PO Box 222
1364   Budapest
Hungary

Contact Mr Andras HIRSCHLER
Tel   361 1181712
Fax   361 1186198

Euro Info Correspondence Centre
Gaza/West Bank Development
Resource Center (DRC)
Industrial Area Erez
PO Box 74
79150   Erez
Israel

Contact Ms Cornelia FRANK
Tel   972 7 863301
Fax   972 7 824275
E-mail   100320.3534@
          compuserve.com

Israel Euro Info Correspondence
Centre
Israel Export Institute
29 Hamered Street
POB 50084
68125   Tel-Aviv
Israel

Contact Mr Yair PERI
Tel   972 3 5142849/889
Fax   972 3 5142852
E-mail   eicc@export.gov.il

Euro Info Correspondence Centre
Jordan Export Development and
Commercial Centers Corporation
(JEDCO)
Shmeisani i Akrama Al-Karashi
PO Box 7704
11118   Amman
Jordan

Contact Mr Kamil MADANAT
Tel   962 6 603507
Fax   962 6 684568
E-mail   jedco@nets.com.jo

EuroMarketing

Euro Info Correspondence Centre
Latvian Development Agency
Perses Street 2
1442   Riga
Latvia

Contact   Mr Juris CINITIS
Tel   371 7283425/7227654
Fax   371 7820458/7282524
E-mail   jcinitis@lda.gov.lv

Euro Info Centre de Correspondance
Chambre de Commerce et d'Industrie
1 rue Justinien – Sanayeh
BP 111801
Beirut
Lebanon

Contact   M Albert NASR
Tel   961 1 744164
Fax   961 1 349615
E-mail   ccib1db@destination.com.lb

Euro Info Correspondence Centre
Vilniaus Narutis/Lithuanian
Association of CCI/Lithuanian
Information Institute
Pilies Street 24
2600   Vilnius
Lithuania

Contact   Mr Saulius SMALYS
Tel   3702 223613/220373
Fax   3702 220580
Web site   www.omnitel.net/leicc/
E-mail   g.alkimavicins@post.omnitel.net.

Euro Info Correspondence Centre
Malta Export Trade Corporation
(METCO)
PO Box 08
SGN 01   San Gwann
Malta

Contact   Dorothy CALLEJA
Tel   356 497560
Fax   356 496687/441106
Web site   www/metco.com.mt

Euro Info Centre de Correspondance
Euro Info Maroc – Centre Européen
pour l'Information des Entreprises
au Maroc
Av Forces Armées Royales 71b
Casablanca
Morocco

Contact   M Abdesslem TAADI
Tel   212 2 447410/11/12
Fax   212 2 447262

Euro Info Centres

Euro Info Correspondence Centre The Cooperation Fund Ul Zurawia 6/12 00-503 Warsaw Poland	Contact Tel Fax E-mail	Mr Ireneusz KAMINSKI 48 22 6251319/1426 48 22 6251290 euroinfo@pirx.cofund. org.pl
Euro Info Centre de Correspondance Chambre de Commerce et d' Industrie de Roumanie 22 boulevard N Balcescu 79502 Bucharest Romania	Contact Tel Fax	M Ioan CIUPERCA 401 3366690/6879 401 3366783
Euro Info Correspondence Centre National Agency for Development of SMEs Nevädzová 5 821 01 Bratislava Slovakia	Contact Tel Fax Web site E-mail	Mr Igor BLÁHA 42 7 237563/231873 42 7 5787342 www.savba.sk/logos/ trade/list.html eicc@nadsme.sanet.sk
Euro Info Centre de Correspondance Office Suisse d' Expansion Commerciale (OSEC) Stampfenbachstrasse 85 8035 Zürich Switzerland	Contact Tel Fax Web site E-mail	Mr Urs LEIMBACHER 41 1 3655454 41 1 3655411 www.osec.ch urs.leimbacher@ ecs.osec.inet.ch
Euro Info Centre de Correspondance Tunisie Agence de Promotion de l'Industrie (API) 63 rue de Syrie 1002 Tunis Tunisia	Contact Tel Fax	M Kefi MOUMNI 216 1 289309 216 1 782482

EuroMarketing

Euro Info Correspondence Centre
SMIDO – Small and Medium Industry
Development Organization
MKEK Binasi, Kat: 11
Tandogan
06330   Ankara
Turkey

Contact   Ms Meral SAYIN
Tel   90 312 2122382
Fax   90 312 2238769
Web site www.kosgeb.gov.tr/eic
E-mail   maf@kosgeb.gov.tr

INDEX

adaptation
   need for 15–16
   of product range 73, 84
advertising 22–3, 104–5, 107, 116
   case examples 32, 33, 49, 122–3
advertising/PR agencies 108–9, 110, 111, 115–16
   case example 32–3
agencies
   case examples 32–3, 61
   market research 65–6, 66–7, 64
   PR/advertising 108–9, 110, 111, 115–16
   sales 28, 95–6, 100
anticipating customer needs 80
Austria, European Information Centres 135–6

Baileys Original Irish Cream Liqueur 48–9
barriers to trade 19, 77–8, 83, 129–30
beer consumption trends 72
Belgium, European Information Centres 137–9
benchmarking 13

border controls 19
brainstorming 43, 45
brand strategies 104–5, 110–11, 115, 117–19
brewery example 71–4
Business Cooperation Network 96
business plans 17
businesses, talking to other 52

carpet cleaner franchising example 123–4
certification requirements *see* technical product standards
chambers of commerce 25, 55, 96
change factors 12, 15
Ciberveu 42–5
clothing contractor example 124–5
coast-to-coast marketing 51–2, 88–9, 120–4
communication activities *see* promotional policies
company taxation 129
competitors 12–13, 39, 50, 53
   question checklists 13, 18, 30, 46, 107

193

Index

researching 39, 53, 54–8, 66
talking to 52
component supplier trends 21
computer company example 98
consultancies *see* agencies
consumer behaviour information 36–7
  beer consumption example 72–3
copyright 132
corporate literature 112
cultural differences 36–7, 111, 127
  case example 76
currency problems 37
customers 36–7, 42–58
  agent recommendations 96
  case examples 42–5, 53–4
  contacting potential 113
  question checklists 30, 46, 107
  researching 54–8, 66, 80
  talking with 50–1, 52–3
  targeting 49–50

Day Runner, Inc. 53
Dell computer company 98–9
Denmark, European Information Centres 140–1
design projects 111–12
design rights 132
developing strategies 120–5
Diekirch 71–4
direct mail 116, 123
directories, trade 57–8
discount strategies 27, 89
distribution documents 102–3
distribution policies 22, 27–8, 40–1, 94–103
  case examples 32–3, 34, 44, 54, 72–3, 99–100
  documents 102–3
  question checklists 29, 101
  US examples 96–9
double taxation agreements 129
DTL 53–4

engineering services example 123
environmental issues 26
Espresso coffee company example 31–4, 87–8
'Euromarketing' concept 11, 31–5
European Information Centres 25, 55
  addresses 135–86
evaluating strategies 120–5
exhibitions, trade 66, 96, 113, 114
export assistance organisations 25, 55, 96

fairs, trade 66, 96, 113, 114
fan distribution example 54
fertiliser company example 122–3
Finland, European Information Centres 142
fitted kitchen company example 74–7
flavourings company example 88
foreign multinationals 20–1
fragmentation, market 76
framework directives 130–1
France, European Information Centres 143–9
franchising 22, 123–4
future business aspirations 16
future developments 127, 133–4

Germany, European Information Centres 150–6
Greece, European Information Centres 157–9

handicapped market example 42–5
Henley Centre for Forecasting 23–4
home market, Europe as 19–20

ICC 81–2
Iceland, European Information Centres 160
identity development 64, 104–5, 109–10
  case examples 32–3, 73, 74

Index

Illy, Riccardo 87–8
Illycaffe 31–4, 87–8
image creation *see* identity development
implementing strategies 120–5
incentives system example 76
industrial shoe company example 81–2
information collection *see* research
innovation, product 42–5, 80
integrated approaches 20, 38–9, 64, 115
　case examples 53–4
intellectual property 131–2
Ireland, European Information Centres 161–2
Irish Dairy Board 104–5
　see also Kerrygold
Italy, European Information Centres 163–8

Kerrygold 67–8, 104–5
kitchen company example 74–7

language issues 51, 67, 111, 114
lawn fertiliser company example 122
legal advice 95
legislation
　Community 15, 19, 133
　national 23, 25, 26, 28, 127
Leite, Teofilo 81
literature, promotional 112
Luxembourg, European Information Centres 169
Luxembourg Convention 132

mailing lists 116, 123
management involvement 125
　personal visits 51, 52–3
market fragmentation 76
market research 47–8, 50–1, 61
　agencies 65–6, 66–7
　case examples 48–9

ongoing 80
reports 57
market segmentation 60–1
market size 16, 18
marketing data sources 57
marketing mix 39
　and positioning 66–7
marketing trends, Europe 20–1
medical diagnostic company example 59–62, 89
missions, trade 96
Mobalpa 74–7
Monster Cable 97–8
Munich Convention 132
mutual recognition 22, 129

national roll outs 52, 98, 120–4
national standards 83, 129–30
Netherlands, European Information Centres 170–1
niche marketing 40, 41, 65
　case examples 61–2, 73, 75, 81
Norway, European Information Centres 172

Oil Changers, Inc. 52
'one market' approach 49
'one' marketing approach 36–41
outside consultants *see* agencies
own company assessment 13, 16–18

Pace, Inc 121–2
packaging 41, 111
Pagh Morup 124–5
pan-European image creation 32–3
parallel imports 89–90
partial standardisation 78
patents 132
Pecheur, Edgar 71, 73
Perlarom 88
personal visits 50–1, 52–3
physical delivery of goods 27
Pie Medical 59–62, 89

195

Index

plans
  business 17
  positioning 65–6
  strategic 126–7
Portugal, European Information Centres 173–5
positioning 39, 59–70
  case examples 59–62, 67–8
  and promotion strategy 110, 117
  and price 40
  questions to ask 63–4
  statements 64–5, 66, 68–70
positioning plans 65–6
positioning statements 64–6
  drafting 68–70
premium pricing 87–8
  advantages 88–9
press releases 113
Preveza 99–100
pricing policies 21–2, 26–7, 40, 87–93
  case examples 76, 89
  and currency 37
  premium 87–9
  question checklist 30, 91–3
  re-imports 89–90
private label goods 22
procurement, public 132–3
product policies 21, 26, 40, 71–86
  case examples 32–3, 71–7
  quality 82–3
  question checklists 29, 79
  research 51, 80
  specialisation 81–2
  standardisation 21, 77–8, 83, 130–1
professional qualification recognition 129
promotional literature 112
  advertising 105, 116
  brand policy 104–5, 110–11, 117–19
  choosing agencies 108–9
  design 111–12
  direct mail 116

public relations 112–14
  question checklists 29, 106–7, 108–9, 117
  sales promotion 115–16
promotional policies 22–3, 28, 41, 104–19
public procurement 132–3
public relations agencies 108–9, 110, 111, 115–16
  case example 32–3
public relations (PR) policies 112–14
  managerial visits 51
publications, trade 113

qualifications, recognition of 129
quality 82–3
  case examples 73, 74, 75–6, 77
  and price 88
quick printing firm example 52

regional market development 20, 84
re-imports 89–90
reorganisation case example 124–5
research 25–30, 39, 42–58, 126
  competitors 39, 53, 54–8, 66
  customers 54–8, 66, 80
  market 47–9, 50–1, 61, 65–6, 80
  positioning 65–7
  question checklist 29–30, 46–7
restrictive clauses 90
retailers, policy variations 41
roll-outs 52, 98, 120–4

sales agents 28, 95–6
  case examples 100
sales agreements, restrictive clauses 90
sales offices 28
sales policies *see* distribution policies
sales promotion 23, 115–16
  case example 76
salsa producer example 121–2
segmentation, market 60–1
seminars 114

196

Index

similarities, looking for product 84
Single Market effects 11, 15–24
  benefits 19–20
  case example 23–4
  disappearing barriers 19
  question checklist 18
  trends 20–3
single marketing strategies 36–41
single pricing policies 89
social research 37, 39
sole agents/distributors 28, 95–6
Spain, European Information Centres 176–80
speaker cable company example 97–8
speaking opportunities 114
specialisation, product 81–2
sponsorship opportunities 114
standardisation
  marketing policies 37–41
  product 21, 32, 33, 77–8, 84
standards, technical product 83, 130–1
statements, positioning 64–6
strategic planning 16–17, 126–7
street lighting company example 53–4
subsidiary operations 94
supplier direct selling 121
Sweden, European Information Centres 181
SWOTS analysis 16

targeting customers 49–50
tax 28
  company 129
  value added 128
'technical barriers to trade' 129–30
technical product standards 83, 130–1
technological innovation 15
teddy bear company example 121
testing positioning statements 65–6
testing requirements *see* technical

product standards
textiles company example 99–100
time planner company example 53
top management involvement 125
  personal visits 51, 52–3
trade associations 25, 55
trade barriers *see* barriers to trade
trade directories 57–8
trade exhibitions/fairs 66, 96, 113, 114
trade marks 131–2
trade missions 96
trade publications 113
training of distributors/agents 95, 97
trends, European marketing 20–1
Tripledge 98

ultrasound scanner company example 59–62
under-pricing 88–9
unified marketing strategies 36–41
United Kingdom, European Information Centres 182–6
USA examples 11, 120–4
  customer/competitor research 51–4
  distribution policies 96–9
  pricing strategies 88–9

value added tax (VAT) 128
Vermont Teddy Bear 121
videos, promotional 113–14
Viladomat, Joseph 42–3
vision projection 111
visits, personal 50–1, 52–3
'voiced thermometers' example 42–5
Vornado Fans 54

windscreen wipers distribution example 98
written research sources 57–8